STOP SABOTAGING YOUR SOBRIETY

STOP SABOTAGING YOUR SOBRIETY

AND CREATE A LIFE YOU LOVE

NICOLE MOLLOY

CONTENTS

CHAPTER 1

YOU ARE NOT BROKEN

know that you're hurting and your soul is tired. There's so much about your past that you wish you could go back and do differently. The memories creep back into your mind to haunt you when you least expect it. The regret. The shame. The guilt.

You're sober now, but you still have this nagging fear in the back of your mind that wonders if you're going to relapse again, destroying everything you've worked so hard for. You know that there's more to life, and you know that you want it; you just don't know how to get it and you can't seem to stop making the same mistakes, over and over again. Something has to change. You just don't know how.

First off, you are NOT broken! Addiction is nothing more than the physical manifestation of pain, sadness, and anger left unexamined for too long--whether conscious or subconscious. Very often, people use drugs and alcohol to try and numb the pain they feel inside, or to quiet their mind, which you know all too well, doesn't work for very long. Feeling emotional pain doesn't mean that you are weak, it means that you are human.

Being stuck in the cycle of addiction is hell on Earth and you don't deserve to live there for another second. You don't deserve to be consumed by the darkness any longer. You might feel like you're barely holding on by a thread. You might feel like a fragile piece of glass that could break at any moment. You might not even truly understand who you are, but I'm here to tell you that after everything you've been through, underneath it all, you are still you. You are still the same beautiful soul that you came into this world as. You are not gone, you've just gotten lost temporarily... and that's okay.

I wrote this book for you so that you can find your way out of the insanity of active addiction once and for all. I want you to want more for yourself than your next fix. I want you to not only see the clouds part, but feel them part within you, revealing a clear blue sky full of beautiful, new opportunities and experiences. I want you to feel as if you've unzipped your old skin, stepped out of it, and tossed it aside, because it just doesn't fit who you are anymore.

I want you to find the courage within you to do the things you most want to do. I want you to feel free from the chains of your past, learn to live in the present, and be excited about the future. I want you to wake up each morning and be thankful for the person you are becoming and love that you are alive to experience every part of it. I want you to laugh again and see the beauty in the most ordinary of moments.

Once you step into your new life, you'll feel a passion burning inside you that will keep you motivated in all that you do, whether that's maintaining your recovery, or planning your next great life adventure. Opportunities will open up simply because you've learned how to open yourself up to them. One day, you'll take a step back and look at your life and be completely overwhelmed, not by sadness and frustration, but with joy and gratitude at how far you've come and how much your life has changed for the better.

CHAPTER 2

MY STORY

When people hear that I've written a book to help addicts, a question I sometimes get asked is "What motivated you to write this book? Why are you so driven to help addicts when you've never been one yourself?" To which I reply, "God motivated me to write this book. The gifts that have been given to me by Him were meant to be shared with everyone. Especially with those who would benefit from them the most. I also know that if I can help an addict to heal and transform their life, then not only do I get to help that one person, I get to heal entire families. My passion is spirituality and psychology, and teaching people how to use both of those things to transform their lives, absolutely fuels my fire. I wrote this book because it hurts me deeply to see people struggle through their lives when I know that they don't have to.

For you, as an addict in recovery, it's important to have people in your life who understand your struggles first hand through their own experiences, but it's also very important to have someone in your life who can guide you and teach you new things, so that you'll continually grow and evolve as a person. Very often, we have to venture outside of our friends and family circle to find what we need in life. That's what I'm here for.

As for my unique gifts, I am an Empath which allows me to feel the emotions of other people on a very profound level. I can feel their pain, their joy, their anxiety, their fears, and their doubts etc. Being able to tune into the good, the bad, and the ugly of people's emotions, gives life such depth and meaning that I wouldn't want to live any other way.

I also possess a psychic level gift known as "Intuitive Claircognizance." This gift allows me to telepathically communicate with my Spirit Guides and Angels who feed me insightful and important information about the world and people. These two gifts combined have allowed me to interpret the world in a way that has saved me a ton of grief and pain in life. I wrote this book to share some of these insights with you, so that you too can use them to save yourself unnecessary pain and suffering.

Each one of us has an important and unique role to play in this lifetime, and people cannot step into this role if they're not sober and living in a way that honors just how special and important they are.

There is no "you" and "me"; there is only "we" and when you are hurting, I am hurting too. We all play an important part in the "collective consciousness" of this human experience. We all need to look out for each other, and be open to accepting help from others when we need it.

While many people judge addicts harshly, I only see beautiful souls that have temporarily gotten lost in life. I know that if a person is strong enough to open their mind and heart to receiving guidance, I can show them how to think and feel differently about themselves and the world we're living in. Anyone can reclaim their power and reclaim their life… they just have to want it and be willing to do the work to get there.

Very often, other people's stories and struggles inspire us and affect our lives in different ways. For example, I have a dear friend named Tara who has been using for twenty years of her life, and trying to get, and stay clean for nine of those years. When I met Tara, my first impression of her was that she was fun, intelligent, beautiful, and funny. It kills me inside when people can't see their own worth and their own beauty.

Tara's main drug of choice was heroin, but she's tried just about everything. She's also tried just about everything to get clean; moving to a new state, countless detoxes, residential treatment, halfway houses, sober houses, methadone, suboxone, but nothing ever worked.

During her last relapse, which lasted for a year, Tara was living with her boyfriend Ray. Tara fell in love with Ray's positivity and dependability. When he said he'd do something, he'd do it. A hard worker with a lust for adventure and a great sense of humor, he was always up for trying something new like surfing, biking, or cooking. They shared a mutual love for each other… and for getting high. While their love was real, their relationship was toxic.

During their time living together they were shooting $1,000 of dope a day. They stayed in bed- bug infested drug houses, not showering for an entire month because all they cared about was their next fix. On two separate occasions, Tara watched Ray overdose and had to revive him with Narcan and CPR. Needless to say, that was very traumatizing for her.

Ray made great money as a fisherman, but they spent it as fast as he made it. At one point they spent $80,000 in a two-month period. Mostly on drugs. Eventually though, Ray couldn't hold down a job anymore and the money completely dried up… and as Tara stated "once the money goes, so do your morals." Tara and Ray took to robbing, cheating, and stealing from people to make ends meet. She sold everything she owned; including her phone and her car. She had absolutely nothing to her name.

To make matters worse, during this time, our mutual friend; Eric, who was one of Tara's best friends, died from a heroin overdose. Eric was a charismatic guy and had so many friends who loved him. He battled addiction for many years and was very open and honest about it. He inspired people with his recovery efforts by being featured on an episode of the A&E television series, Intervention. Eric tried incredibly hard to stay sober, but after four years of dancing in and out of sobriety, the disease eventually caught up with him, and he passed away on August 19, 2017.

Talking with Tara outside of Eric's wake, I could see that she was visibly shaken by his death. She knew that she could be the next to die, but still couldn't stop herself from getting high before his wake in order to try and numb the barrage of emotions she was feeling that day.

Shortly thereafter, Tara and Ray were served eviction papers. She was spiraling into a deep depression. Waking up each morning, angry that she didn't die in her sleep. Sick of being dope sick every 6 hours from the fentanyl. Everything of value was gone: no car, no job, no money, no phone, no place to live, no hustle left in her, no hope whatsoever. Walking the streets doing things she's ashamed to admit. Things like prostitution, which she vowed she'd never do. Trauma upon trauma. Her soul was exhausted. She knew something had to change.

In November of 2017, Tara entered a long-term inpatient treatment program alone, without Ray. She was lost, and felt so broken inside, but she was ready to make changes within herself that would transform her life. She decided that she was done with the secrets. Done with the lies. For the first time ever, she became honest with herself and others.

She realized that she was using in order to numb her emotions. Emotions that stem from the fact that she couldn't stand to be alone with herself, and that there was always an endless void within her that she was never able to fill. She didn't love herself and felt completely alone. She felt unworthy of love because growing up she had a mother who didn't know how to show compassion and love toward her and it drove her insane.

One day, during her time in the treatment program, Tara was overcome with sadness and couldn't stop crying. She had a feeling that something was wrong with Ray. Not knowing how to get in touch with him at the time, she called his Mother, who had just learned the devastating news from the Police that Ray's body had been found in an abandoned house. Ray, Tara's boyfriend of seven years, was dead.

Tara always said to herself that if Ray died, she was going to overdose and die with him, but that just wasn't an option for her anymore. Sitting at his funeral, watching Ray's son carry his Father's casket, ignited a fire within her to make a real, lasting change and choose life. From that point on she refused to be another statistic, or a RIP Facebook post.

Tara made a decision right then and there to learn more about herself and develop her spirituality and connection with God. When asked which recent changes within herself were having the greatest impact on her ability to stay sober, she said that she prays every day, and that she's stopped feeling sorry for herself and wanting sympathy from others. She believes in herself and respects herself. She's honest, kind, and respectful of others, and tries to help people in need. She's completely removed toxic people from her life and has added people in who support and inspire her. She's learned to accept God's will and has the willingness and desire to keep going and growing. Tara is learning what it means to truly love herself, and that is changing her life in unimaginable ways. Tara has been sober for a year and a half now, and is thriving. She's living in a sober home that she loves, is working full time, and has gone back to school.

There's immeasurable power that comes from having the right people in your life, and the right information at

---

the right time; which is why I wrote this book, and why I'm so passionate about helping addicts in recovery to develop a healthy relationship with God and themselves. It's truly life changing, and you deserve to experience it too.

Our childhood experiences shape who we are and set the foundation for our future. Growing up, I could see that my parents were complete opposites. My Mother, a quiet, gentle soul who worked in nursing, would do anything, for anyone. Slim with dark hair and loving brown eyes, she, to a fault, always put everyone else's needs before her own. My Father was a rough, gruff, truck driver by day and Harley Davidson mechanic by night. Bearded, burley, and covered in tattoos, he was always angry about something.

He lived the full-blown biker lifestyle and spent most of his time away from home drinking and drugging with his friends. He wasn't incredibly involved in my growth and development, and much like Tara's Mother, he didn't know how to show love and affection.

Around the age of ten is when my Spirit Guides and Angels began speaking to me very audibly in the form of telepathy, which is the exchange of knowledge from one mind to another without speaking. In the psychic world this is known as Claircognizance, or "clear knowing" because it feels like an exchange of information with full understanding. Like a cosmic download of sorts.

I remember watching my Father fearfully one day as he was yelling about something and suddenly, out of the blue, a voice spoke to me very clearly and said, "he doesn't understand how he's hurting people right now, but he will one day, be patient with him and don't take anything he says or does personally."

This voice not only resonated in my head, but in my heart with full understanding, and over the years to come, I never took anything my Father said or did (or didn't do) personally… or any other human for that matter, because I understood from that moment on, that we're all imperfect, and we're all learning, and we're all at different stages of what we can understand.

I chose to forgive and love my Father regardless of his shortcomings because I knew he loved me as much as he possibly could, with who he was at that point in his life. There was nothing I, or anyone else, could do to speed up his soul's wisdom and maturity, because that was up to him and God to work on over time. All I could do, was step back and respect the process.

This experience allowed me to still love my Father, but love him from a healthy distance while "holding space" for him to grow. We all need to hold space for the people we love to grow and mature without allowing them to cause us emotional pain. It's a mind blowing moment once you realize that your parents aren't superheroes, but simply people like you and me who are dealing with their own personal issues, and are trying to figure it all out too.

We also need to learn how to hold space for ourselves, and our own personal growth, without judging ourselves harshly for being imperfect. If we beat ourselves up for failing, we'll never dare to grow again, and that in itself is a self-sabotaging behavior.

It's important to remember that in our own struggle to find and love ourselves, our story inadvertently becomes other people's story as well. Pain is easily passed down from generation to generation and from person to person, so the sooner we can heal and learn to protect ourselves, the sooner we can put an end to the cycle of hurt.

In fact, when a member of a family decides to wake up and take notice of the destructive patterns that are being passed down, by healing themselves, they'll also heal the present day generation, the souls of the generations before them, and the future generations to come. This is a very honorable role to play within a family because it helps so many people. Could you be this person for your family?

Ever since I was a young child, spirituality has intrigued me. Being that I connected so easily to the other side, I never doubted that there is more to life than this Earthly world we're living in now. I just knew automatically that something more existed.

I was raised Catholic and around the age of 15 is when the church asks you to make your confirmation and proclaim to the world that you are choosing to be of the Catholic faith from this point on in your life, for the rest of your life. I was pretty certain that I was going to go through with it. I attended the retreat they make you go to, and at the end of the day they handed out the gowns you're supposed to wear on the day of the ceremony.

The next day I decided to try the gown on to make sure it fit. Standing in front of my full-length mirror in my bedroom I zipped up the white gown and stretched my arms out to each side of me. The arms of the sleeves hung long and low making me look like some kind of holy wizard. My jaw dropped and a thought came rushing over me that I couldn't ignore. "What if I'm in a cult? What if I haven't questioned anything about what I've been taught my whole life? I can't go through with this." I ran downstairs to tell my Mother about the choice I made not to make my confirmation. I was a little afraid to break the news to her, because there she was standing at the counter making the appetizers for the party we were planning to have the next day. She looked stunned and replied "You're going to break your Grandmother's heart. You have to call her and tell her." My heart sank, but I knew that what I was doing was right. I knew that questioning the answers I was fed my entire life was the responsible thing to do.

I called my Grandmother on the phone (a.k.a., "Grammy") and she didn't say much. I could tell she was hurt, being a devout Catholic herself, but I think she understood that this was a journey I needed to go on. A journey to figure out the truth of what really exists on the other side. Why we're really here, who's in charge, and what the point of life really is. I told myself that I was going to take some time to investigate different religions and schools of thought before I'd make a decision. So that's what I set out to do. I was on a mission.

For the record, I do not feel that the Catholic faith is a cult. In fact, I've found it to make a lot of sense; but at the same time, a lot of it also doesn't make any sense. I feel the same way about many other religions.

Through the years, the things I've learned on my spiritual journey have increased my understanding of God and the Universe and who He really is. My spirituality is best described as a patchwork quilt, created with beautifully shaped concepts of God and life that have been stitched together in a unique way that makes sense to me as it pertains to all of humanity.

When I was around the age of 12, my Grandmother took me to a place called La Salette Shrine. La Salette is a Christian based destination where the public can go to feel closer to God. It has gorgeous gardens and water fountains and in the winter months they put on an impressive display of Christmas lights. Grammy would take me there from time to time as a child to enjoy a beautiful day where I'd be exposed in a lighthearted way to the messages of God.

That particular day, after spending time in the gardens, we decided it was time to head back to the car and go home. On the way out, Grammy recognized a Nun that she knew who worked there. We walked up to her and they began to chat. As I was standing there, their conversation caught my attention and then the Nun turned directly to me and said "I'm not afraid to die because I've died before and I know what it's like on the other side and it's incredibly beautiful." Astonished, I questioned her "You died?" "Yes, she said with a smile, and I didn't want to come back because it was so beautiful and peaceful there, but I'll go back someday. So for now I just have to be patient."

Little did I know at the time, that many years later, near death experience (NDE) stories like this would come to play an important role in my discovery and belief of who we are, why we're here, and the meaning of life.

So what is it that I do exactly? Just as they would hire a nutritionist or personal trainer to improve their physical health, people can hire me as a Spiritual Wellness Mentor to improve their emotional health. I want to teach you what I've learned through the years about spirituality, mindful thinking, and self-sabotaging behavior, and help you to apply it to your own life. I want to help you to view yourself, the world, and God differently so that you can create a life full of joy, peace, courage, strength, and love. I want you to consider me a friend who is here to guide you through the complicated process of self-discovery and healing. When you're ready to take your spirituality and self-awareness to the next level and transform your life, I'll be here. Just reach out.

CHAPTER 3

OUR JOURNEY TOGETHER

Together, we'll embark on a journey of enlightenment that will transform both your mind and your spirit. After years of trying to figure it all out on your own, your soul is undoubtedly craving the clarity that this knowledge will bring. It's hungry to devour the information it needs so that both your brain and your heart can become aligned with one another and therefore be more open to connecting with the Higher Power (which I call God).

Once this happens, it's a feeling like no other because with it comes a powerful new sense of self-confidence and strength to stand your ground. It will help you to understand the bigger picture of life and will completely change your perception of God. It will reactivate the divine compass inside your heart so that you no longer feel lost in your decision making. It will help you to learn to love yourself and the process of inward reflection, and will inspire you to bravely plan your future with a passion and purpose that will make the experience of living this life enjoyable and exciting.

A quick little side note--I want you to own this book. I mean REALLY own it! Not simply by buying it and reading it, but by not being afraid to mark it all up! Find a yellow highlighter and a pen and highlight the things you read that really resonate with you so that you don't forget them. Take a pen and write your questions in the margins and direct message me on Facebook or Instagram with them. I want this to be an interactive experience for us. Now you'll really be able to dive into each chapter with passion! And if something you read causes your mind to wander and think about things in the context of your own life, allow yourself time to contemplate. Thinking deeply is how we grow and change for the better.

Our journey begins in Chapter 4 with a Spirituality 101 lesson where I hope to teach you some of the things that organized religion has kept a secret from the masses for so long. This is where I'm going to tell you about the coolest things I've learned throughout my spiritual journey. I hope that this will create a solid spiritual base for your growth that will remove any confusion about why we're born and the purpose of life. We'll also take a look at who God really is…. because He is greatly misunderstood by almost all of humanity. It's a good thing He's very patient.

Next, in Chapter 5, I want to talk to you about how incredibly special you are and how important it is that you're here on this planet at this exact moment in time. We'll talk about what it means to live on a higher level and getting to know your true "higher self" by becoming your own best friend.

The next two lessons in Chapters 6 and 7 teach the basics of how to create a mindful heart and a mindful mind. There are several points within each lesson that will help you to fully understand the concepts so that you can begin to implement each one of them into your life. These points will play a vital role in helping you to navigate your life moving forward.

Then we move on to Chapter 8. At this point, you will have learned so much more about God, the world, and yourself than you know now, so I feel that you'll be ready to journey a little deeper and take an honest look inwards at yourself. This is a very exciting part of the book because the gold nuggets of our own truths are buried deeply within us… and once you uncover them, feel them, and free them, your spirit will feel richer, renewed, and more alive than ever before.

In Chapter 9, we'll dive into evaluating and learning about your thoughts, feelings, and behaviors as they relate to helping you to stay sober in the moments when you feel tempted to use again. If you ever feel weak, you'll have a collection of insights and knowledge in your arsenal to combat the tidal wave of emotions that threaten to push you down. In moments like these, you'll have the power you need to be the captain of your own ship and weather the storm.

Then, in Chapter 10, we'll move on to talk about passion and purpose and how to begin discovering your own unique talents and passions. Every single one of us are given special gifts by God that we're supposed to share with the world. Finding out what those are is such a fun and exciting journey in itself because it encourages you to think even more deeply about who you are, what you want to experience in your life, and what's most important to you.

Then comes Chapter 11, where we'll talk about the importance of keeping daily rituals. I cannot tell you how critical it is that you make your newfound spirituality and mindfulness a part of your everyday life. The greater your commitment to making time to check in with yourself and God each day, the easier it will become to do this automatically, and eventually, you'll come to crave the time you get to spend in peaceful reflection, because in the stillness and calm, you'll find the meaning, answers, and direction you've been seeking your whole life. Silence and solitude will no longer be a scary thing for you.

So if you're ready to get going, let's get started on the first lesson!

CHAPTER 4

LESSON 1:
WHAT ORGANIZED RELIGION DOESN'T TELL US

For one reason or another, many people have decided to shun organized religion. As a result of doing this they often feel as if they are not allowed to have a relationship with God--and nothing could be further from the truth; because God is not found in a church, God is found within yourself. You carry Him with you everywhere, no matter where you go. God wants to be your friend. He wants to be your guide. He wants to help you navigate your way through the hard times, and yes, He even wants you to put all of your anger, stress, disappointment, and confusion onto Him so that He can deal with it and you don't have to. How many friends do you have in your life right now that want to bear your deepest burdens for you? Probably not too many; so your relationship with God is something very special.

Who is God? For me, God is the same energy no matter what name you decide to call Him: The Higher Power, The Universe, Yahweh, Jah, Jehovah, Yeshua, Allah,

Elohim, the list goes on and on and on. It's such a shame that so many wars have been fought over religion, when both sides are defending the same exact energetic being. I sometimes imagine God looking at humanity and doing a big "facepalm." We'll get into greater detail about who and what God is throughout the book. For now though, let's take a look at what organized religion doesn't want you to know about life and the afterlife.

When you die, and your soul leaves your body and travels back to the other side, you will meet God. As you're standing there basking in the warm, comforting, spectacularly overwhelming feeling of His unconditional love, you will be asked the most important question of your entire life… "Did your soul learn the lessons it set out to learn during your lifetime?"

What I'm about to tell you has been experienced by thousands upon thousands of people around the globe each year who have had a near death experience (NDE). Their experiences are strikingly similar to one another in some ways, and unique to their own soul's growth in other ways. The knowledge that people gain when they have these experiences is extraordinary and life changing. Even the complete skeptics who didn't believe in God, come back total believers and forever changed.

Regarding the spiritual journey I told you about earlier in the book, I've learned quite a bit over the years about NDE's and I want to share this knowledge with you because I believe it to be the unfiltered truth of what the purpose of life (and death) is really about.

The next thing that happens to a person as they are standing there with God is that they are presented with a look back on their entire life. Surprisingly, many have said that their life played back to them as if it were on a movie or television-like screen that came out of nowhere. As long and drawn out as life feels to us here on Earth, near death experiencers (NDE'ers) say that it didn't take long to review their entire life--from birth, through childhood, adolescence, young adulthood, through to adulthood--they were able to understand their entire life as one single event.

While reviewing your life you will relive all of the moments that your actions caused people joy, and all of the moments that your actions caused people pain; either on purpose or by mistake. This is done so that your soul completely understands the impact that your life had on others while you were alive. The only way to truly learn in life is through experience; so if you caused people pain, you will feel their pain just as they felt it. If you caused people joy; you will feel their joy just as they felt it.

All the big and the small things you did throughout your life will be reviewed and experienced. Even the seemingly insignificant things you did, like that time you held the door open with a smile for a stranger, will be relived. You will feel the happiness you created for that person, because in that moment you made them feel seen and special. You will feel all of it. You'll begin to realize that there are no small acts of kindness, because every little thing you do has an impact on the world around you that is far greater than you could ever imagine.

This is just one reason why everything you do in this world should be done with love in mind, because you will have to experience it again one day, and hey... I'd rather experience a bunch of joy, than a bunch of pain any day. As for feeling the pain you caused others during your life review, this is not something to worry about. We all have to experience this. There's no way around it because there are no perfect people. NDE'ers have described this part of their life review not as being done in a punishing way, but in a factual, "this information is for your own good and growth" type of way. The life review takes only seconds, but the amount of information that is conveyed to your soul in that short amount of time is extraordinary.

The mind blowing part about this life review process is how God is not the one judging us, we end up judging ourselves! God watches us lovingly as we learn our lessons and grow, and he is happy and proud of us for the progress we make during our lifetime. Just think about how this changes everything. So many people are taught by organized religion to live in fear of an angry, wrathful God. One that judges us for the wrongs we have done in our lifetime and will damn us to the fiery pits of Hell for being anything less than perfect--but that's definitely not how it works. One day, when you finally make it back to the other side, God will be there and He'll feel like home, and He'll feel like love, and He'll be happy to see you again, no matter how you chose to live your life on Earth.

What I have to tell you next is very controversial to some people. Another thing that organized religion doesn't teach us is how this is not the only lifetime you will live, or have lived. You have lived many lifetimes before the one you are living right now, and you will live many more to come until your soul finally "gets it." Living multiple lives, one right after the other, is known as reincarnation.

To try and explain the evolution of a person's soul, it's best to visualize it. Have you ever been to Home Depot and seen the paint swatches in the paint department? Let's imagine that I've picked out a bunch of swatches that range from the blackest, black, to the purest white ever created. In between these two colors would be a very diverse range of grey tones that would span from very dark greys, to medium greys, to light greys and then it would move into the white spectrum of colors. I want you to picture that this paint swatch has hundreds of different color levels to it. This is a great way to visualize the path our souls are on and how they must evolve. On one end, the darkest, deepest black color represents pure evil and on the far other end, the purest, brightest white color represents God's pure, unconditional love for everyone and everything. It is the goal of our soul to learn the lessons we need to learn during our lifetimes to move our soul away from darkness and evil, as close as we can to God's white light until eventually we become God-like and have the same level of understanding that God has. Life is like obtaining a doctorate degree for the soul...only it takes a lot longer to graduate from soul school.

Let's talk more about this white light for a minute because it's far more than the kind of light we see with our eyes here on Earth.

God is love. It's the actual thing that God is made of. When NDE'ers reflect back on meeting Him, every single one of them struggle to find the words to express how overwhelming, healing, and incredibly beautiful it felt to be in His loving presence. Most of the time, one of the first things people see and feel when they begin to cross over is "the light" and this light gets brighter, warmer, and more intense the closer people get to it. They describe it as being the brightest light they've ever seen, but how at the same time, it didn't hurt their eyes. Some people have even said that it had a golden or pinkish tone to it.

Other people recount that before their soul experienced this light, it first had to undergo a massive healing. In order to do that, they were brought into a healing realm where they experienced being in a womb-like state in a sea of darkness with a very peaceful feeling to it and a texture like velvet. Then when they were ready, they were able to move toward the light and complete the process of fully crossing over.

Here's how it works in a nutshell. God is the creator of the Universe, and therefore the Universe is God. God's energy is pure, unconditional love, and therefore the energy of the Universe is nothing less, and nothing more, than pure, unconditional love. Just as God created the Universe, He also created each one of us, and therefore we too are simply an extension of God Himself and we are also made of unconditional love. This means that love is the only thing that is real in the world, despite what we were taught to believe growing up. Anything besides love is just noise that humans have created in their own minds out of fear.

The highest vibration a person and their soul can operate at is unconditional love. This is why it's so important that we do all we can to transform our lives into something that honors and mirrors God's unconditional love and light. We can do this by committing to live our life in a way that allows us to "Be the Light" for ourselves and for others by learning to deeply love ourselves and others.

It's important to remember that "like attracts like." You know the saying "misery loves company?" Well, the same is true for love. The energy of love always attracts more love. So when we operate out of love, we attract even more love and goodness into our lives in the form of the thoughts we think, the people we meet, and the opportunities that come into our lives. This is because energy wants to connect with energy that it recognizes and feels comfortable with and therefore is drawn to. So the question to ask yourself right now is "What do I want more of in my life, more good or more bad?" Then actually make a decision to live life in a way that will bring that to you.

Now let's go back a bit and talk more about the lessons our souls needs to learn. When you die, and all of your family and closest friends die too, you will all reconvene again on the other side, because Spirit Families never truly separate. There may be moments of time where we need to live our lives as humans without them, but we'll always meet up with them again in our true home; Heaven.

The people in your life who mean the most to you, or who have had the greatest impact on your life are members of your Spirit Family. There are even members of your Spirit Family who you haven't met yet because they passed on before you were born. Regardless, we'll all meet again on the other side.

As we discussed earlier, when you cross over, God will ask you one question, "Did your soul learn the lessons it set out to learn during your lifetime?" You see, before we're even born, each one of us makes a soul contract with God to learn specific lessons that will bring us closer and closer to the understanding we need to possess in order to become more "God-like." (Remember the paint swatch example I gave earlier?)

The only way we can learn these important lessons is to experience them through living a physical existence in human form, and the lessons we need to learn are done so through our relationships with other people. This is where it gets even more interesting. After you've spent some time relaxing, healing, and having fun in Heaven, you and your Spirit Family eventually decide that it's time to return to Earth to have another human experience in order to learn even more lessons. This is not done in a dreadful way, because when we're in Heaven, our souls are excited to learn more because they know that gaining these experiences will bring us closer to God. God makes us feel so good inside that we crave a deeper connection to Him and are willing to do anything in order to get even closer. This includes going through the emotional pain we need to experience as humans in order to learn these vital lessons.

Having decided to give life another go, you, your Spirit Family, God, and your Angels collectively get together to draft up everyone's perfect life map. This includes all of the lessons that each one of you need to learn in the next lifetime, and assigns the roles that each one of you will play in each other's lives.

Here's another mind-blowing realization. Even a person you dislike here on Earth may actually be a part of your Spirit Family, having volunteered to play the role of someone you consider an "enemy," so that your soul may have the opportunity to learn forgiveness. If we stay open- minded to looking at things this way, then we should live in soulful gratitude to the people and things that hurt us the most because without them we wouldn't have the opportunity to grow!

There is one caveat to all of this though, and that is the gift of freewill that God gives us. Freewill allows us the ability to choose whether or not we learn our lessons. God gives us freewill because he loves us. Without the freewill to learn, we'd simply be robots doing what God com- mands, and where would the lesson be in that? In order for us to learn the lessons that we need to learn, we must choose to want to learn them, and then we must choose to do the work to learn them, and then we must prove that we want to learn them by putting what we have come to understand into action in our own lives. There are a mul- titude of virtues and ways of thinking that a person must master before they can truly understand what it means to be the full embodiment of God's unconditional love and light. Between chapters 6 and 7, we'll dive deeply into what some of those lessons are.

I want to provide you with a sincere warning when choosing not to learn your lessons though. When the time comes for God to ask you if you learned the lessons your soul set out to learn in this lifetime, if your answer is "no," then you must repeat the same exact lessons in your next lifetime, plus your next round of lessons on top of that. So your next lifetime stands to be even more stressful and complicated if you don't take personal responsibility for your soul's growth right now during this lifetime.

A similar experience exists for people who commit suicide, because they're essentially "dropping out of school" early and therefore never get to finish learning their soul lessons. People who commit suicide do not get damned to Hell, they simply have to start all over again in their next lifetime. Which personally, I think is a certain kind of Hell in itself. So if you are feeling desperate, please think twice about killing yourself and don't even consider it an option. Please think twice about being complacent in life and not doing the work you need to do in order to better yourself as a person, because you will regret it one day once you realize you have to live your struggles all over again as if it were Groundhog Day repeating itself over and over again. (Such a great movie!)

Have you ever met someone whose life seems inordinately hard to the point where it doesn't even seem fair?

This is quite possibly because in past lifetimes they refused to learn their lessons and therefore their lessons have piled up, one on top of another, and they have a lot of work to do to in order to catch up.

I would like to invite you to consider something for a moment. What if your personal experience with addiction is the culmination of many lifetimes of unlearned lessons combined into one massive experience? What if your soul specifically chose this path on purpose because it knew that you could get all of your past-due lessons out of the way through this one very challenging hardship, if only you could find the strength to dig deep and untangle the mess of thoughts in your head and find divine clarity through learning what you need to learn. What if you're not reading this book by chance? What if I am a part of your Spirit Family and we worked it out before we were even born that I would be there to guide you through your lessons if and when your soul was ready to grow? I believe this to be the truth. The question is, do you believe it too?

CHAPTER 5

LESSON 2:
LIVING ON A HIGHER LEVEL

There is a term that I'd like to introduce you to called "higher self." This is when a person becomes very connected to, and aware of the truth of their eternal soul and their soul's mission in life. In turn, when people connect with their higher self, they live their life in a higher state of consciousness or awareness. This allows them to better understand themselves, others and the world around them. It is my wish for you that you embrace living life as your higher self because it's such a beautiful and peaceful way to live.

Many people begin using drugs and alcohol as a form of escape from the confusion and chaos of life here on Earth, but if you truly want to escape the human BS, all you need to do is decide that from this point on, you're going to commit to expanding your consciousness a little each day by always striving to learn something new that will bring you closer to God's love and light-- expanding your understanding of the bigger picture and your place in it.

When you choose to live as your higher self, you are making a conscious choice to live life above the noise and chaos of human life. This in itself is a form of escape, but it's a healthy form of escape which allows your enlightened soul to be the one in the driver's seat of your life--not your chaotic human emotions. Emotions are complicated and they are often created by the archaic human "reptilian brain" out of fear and confusion. Once you realize that all that "human stuff" is a waste of your time and energy, and you only live by what governs God's love and light, you'll feel like you've unlocked some kind of mysterious code to the Universe and your life will become peaceful and uncomplicated.

Not only that, you'll come to realize that living "within the code" opens up doors of opportunity for you that you never thought possible. God's Universe responds to the energy we put out into the world. If we're continually putting out energy that is based in fear, then we will get more results that mirror that fear, which are usually negative. If we live in His love, completely devoid of fear, then our energy communicates with God and His Universe that we completely trust God's plan and are open to receiving the abundance of blessings that were already ours to begin with, that have been waiting for us the entire time as part of God's master plan for our lives. The opposite of love isn't hate, it's fear, and you can't live in God's love if you don't let go of fear, and trust that He will protect and guide you at all times.

When NDE'ers are on the other side, many of them claim to be given all of the answers, to all of the questions that have ever been asked by mankind. They claim that in this "all knowingness" they automatically possessed all of the knowledge of the Universe as if it were a complete download of information to their consciousness. Many of these people who were sent back to their bodies because it was not yet their time, claim that this "all knowingness" dissolved from their memory as soon as they returned to their bodies. Some people even recall physically feeling it disappear from their minds, and while they don't remember specific details, they do remember that the answers to life's greatest questions were unbelievably simple.

The fact that complete knowledge is given to us when we're in Heaven, but that it's taken away from us when we come into the human world, tells me loud and clear that we're not supposed to have all of the answers. If we had all of the answers there would be no discovery, and life is most definitely about exploration. God doesn't just want to give us the answers, He wants to give us wisdom, and wisdom is only gained when a person understands something on a deep, personal level through experience or effort.

Be patient with yourself when you don't have all the answers, and don't let your mind run away with a million questions that will only end up causing you undue anxiety. Simply ask God the questions you have, then have faith that the answers you seek will be presented to you in due time when you are meant to receive them. As you are praying, be sure to release and hand over to God any negative emotions that your questions are causing you. Feel within you those emotions exiting your body, leaving your soul completely cleansed. Keep working on gaining knowledge and bettering yourself a little more each day and everything will fall into place as it should.

Now I want to talk about that tricky little thing that ALL humans struggle with called "self-love." I truly believe that we are supposed to struggle with this, simply for the specific act of achieving it. For instance, if God gave us the answers to all the questions we have, we wouldn't truly appreciate the answers. I believe that God wants us to do the work we need to do in order to love ourselves, so that that we can truly appreciate ourselves and our souls for who and what we are. After all, humans don't respect things that are handed to them without having to work for them.

So what this means is that your life is *supposed to be* a journey of self-discovery, and since each one of our souls is literally a little piece of God Himself, in discovering yourself more and more, you'll discover God more and more. This is also a bit of a "What came first, the chicken or the egg?" type thing. Should you learn to love yourself first, then God, or God first then yourself?

The two can, and should be, nurtured at the same time. Both will help the other to grow. So please, if you are hesitant to embrace your relationship with God, I'm going to ask you to reconsider that right now because not doing so will be a complete waste of your time. God is the creator, and his energy is unconditional love, and therefore there's no possible way for humans to truly love themselves in a healthy way without connecting back into the power source that we all originally came from. Which is God, or simply, love. This is what it means when people say "God is love." Because He *is* what love is.

When you live in love, you are living on a higher level. Love for yourself, love for others, love for the world that God created and love for God Himself. If you want the truth, and want all human chaos and drama to lose its power over you, you need to operate on a higher level, as your higher self, and that cannot occur if you're trying to replace the lack of God's love within you with other things like drugs, drinking, shopping, sex, gossip, social media, TV, video games, etc. Nothing external will ever be able to heal the void within you because it doesn't operate in divine truth. Love is the only universal truth. Plain and simple.

So many people who struggle to love themselves are not aware of one essential truth, which is that YOU ARE ALREADY PERFECT! You were created by God and born into this world the most perfect being; non-judgmental, forgiving, gentle, and open to giving and receiving love. Any guilt, shame, remorse, or self-loathing that you may feel toward yourself at this point in your life, stems from lies that you learned to believe about yourself as you were growing up, unintentionally taught to you by your family and the rest of society.

These lies that begin to seep into our minds and take the form of truths are created from a mix of behaviors and feedback that we receive from other humans such as parents or teachers.

Unfortunately, when we are just children, we're at the mercy of the people who raise us. The influence they have on us is absolutely incredible. Although our parents might have meant well at the time, unless they've put a ton of work into growing their spirituality, emotional intelligence, and mindfulness, chances are that the fears and beliefs they learned growing up, inadvertently got passed on to you.

Let's break it down a bit more so you can understand what's actually going on inside of your brain, because once you understand why it behaves the way it does, you'll be able to forgive yourself for simply being human.

One of the first things we do as humans when we're born is begin to gather information about the world to try and make sense of who we are. The only people who can provide us with this information are our caretakers and so we look to them to give us feedback about whether what we're doing is good or bad, approved of or not. We look to our parents as the end all, be all, deciding factor of what is correct or incorrect. They clap and cheer when we do good. They scold disapprovingly when we do wrong. We learn to love the feeling we get when we receive approval, and learn to hate how we feel when we receive disapproval.

Receiving disapproval can do a few different things to a person, it can make us want to stay far, far away from things that would be deemed "wrong" or "bad," which could end up turning us into "people pleasers" or perfectionists. This in turn, creates unrealistic expectations that we can never live up to, which then causes us to never feel good enough.

Receiving disapproval can also make us feel that we are "bad," simply because we received that feedback as a child. Even if we were called "bad" because we threw our spaghetti against the wall, we, as children, at such a young age, don't understand *why* we were bad, only *that* we were bad. Some people go through life believing that they are a "bad person" and it becomes their core identity. This causes them to turn any feedback they receive throughout their life, good, bad, or indifferent, into further confirmation that they are indeed a "bad person." You could give them a compliment and they wouldn't hear it. Give them constructive criticism and they'll take it and twist its meaning, using it to confirm what they've always believed about themselves, that they are "bad." The belief that they are a bad person, and therefore not good enough, stays with them and effects every aspect of their life. Sometimes this belief is openly held and understood by a person, and sometimes it exists on a subconscious level.

On top of that, many parents have their own set of issues, and therefore aren't the least bit aware of the trauma they may be causing in their own children's lives. Any hurt they cause, no matter how extreme, is often not done on purpose, but stems from their own childhood trauma and current ignorance, and therefore shouldn't be taken personally.

This "pass down" of trauma is called "ancestral trauma." This is when trauma from previous generations, gets passed down from generation to generation. Sometimes entire families become blind to the fact that there's anything wrong at all, until one person in the family becomes enlightened enough to see things for what they are, and is brave enough to be the one to stop the pattern from repeating and harming future generations.

This one person in the family who changes themselves, actually ends up healing thousands of people; the souls of their ancestors, souls of future generations, and the souls of those who would have been effected by the "ripple effect" of those actions if left unhealed. Will you be the brave person to step up and do this for you and your family?

So as you can see, the chances of any person making it though childhood truly believing that they're good enough, doesn't seem very promising. There is something incredible happening in the world right now though. There's an energetic shift occurring where a massive collection of people whose consciousness is waking up more and more every single day to the reality that we are all souls derived from the same source, on a mission of transformation while here on this planet. A mission to get closer to God's love and light by living it. By learning our lessons, learning to love ourselves, others, the Earth and God Himself more. We're awakening to the fact that in addition to embracing all of this, we also have to do what we can to help others during their journey as well.

I believe that the human brain was purposefully wired to interpret our childhood feedback as it does, specifically for the process of unlearning all of the lies that hold us back. Once you learn how to love yourself your life will begin to change for the better because you'll be able to openly invite the things into your life that you know you deserve, like love, and success, and happiness. And once a person truly believes that they deserve to experience these things, that's when it will actually begin to happen for them.

You are not alone, We're all a little nervous. We're all a little scared. We're all a little lost, and that's how it's supposed to be. You can be scared and brave at the same time. In fact, courage wouldn't exist without fear. When you find yourself feeling fearful, instead of giving in to that fear, take a moment and thank your fear for giving you the opportunity to understand what strength and courage really means. You can use this technique to turn any "weakness" you might be feeling into a strength.

Never doubt the power you have to change your life by becoming the master of your own thoughts, emotions, and actions. This world is not static and unchanging. Your life is literally your creation.

It's time to be your own best friend and live life on a higher level as your higher self. It's time to acknowledge that you are enough because you came from God. God is perfect and therefore you were born perfect. You never actually stopped being perfect, you only stopped believing that you were. You are perfect in all of your imperfections because imperfections help us to learn and to grow and move closer to God. Instead of letting the challenges in your life overwhelm you, embrace them as opportunities to become an even better version of yourself than you were yesterday. That is the exciting part of life; each day is a new opportunity to transform into the person you most want to become.

CHAPTER 6

LESSON 3:
DIVINE VIRTUES

So what are these lessons that I've been talking about? Well, they come in the form of Divine Virtues and Modalities of Mindful Thinking based off of those virtues. Put together, they create peace, calm, confidence, and joy for the person who commits to live life by this code.

In this chapter we'll examine 8 Divine Virtues, and in the next chapter we'll dive into learning about 4 Mindful Modalities. The Virtues focus on the ways in which God wishes for us to live and the Modalities focus on the way God wishes for us to think in order to avoid self-sabotage and to become a vehicle for His love and light for ourselves and others during our time on this planet.

If you keep these Virtues and Modalities in your heart at all times, they'll end up becoming the foundation of your moral compass and influence all of your decision making in such a way, that you'll always end up making the right choices in life. After all, a person's life is created by all of the collective decisions they'll make throughout their lifetime.

ONE: FORGIVENESS

First, let's define forgiveness; forgiveness is the act of completely separating yourself emotionally from an event in your life that has hurt you in some way, so that it no longer has any control over you.

Forgiveness is one of the hardest things for humans to do, which I find interesting because it's one of the quickest ways to transform your life and the lives of others. This says to me that people have a tough time doing several things: not taking things personally, being non-judgmental, letting the past go, and controlling their emotions.

Mastering the Divine Virtue of forgiveness will bring so much joy and personal power into your life. Imagine living in a world where you love yourself so much that you can forgive yourself for being human and making mistakes, and do the same for others too. Imagine how good other people will feel in your presence when they realize that you understand and accept their humanness by not expecting perfection. Even if someone doesn't acknowledge, reciprocate, or accept your forgiveness, you do not need their approval because we do not forgive for the sake of others. We forgive for ourselves and to release ourselves from the negative emotions that holding onto anger and resentment causes (not to mention the physical ailments that are caused by stress). True joy comes when you learn how to detach from the negative stories you tell yourself about the events in your life. This narrative can work one of two ways; for you, or against you, and it's a choice that you make by choosing your thoughts.

Not being able to forgive yourself and others is the quickest way to create an environment within yourself that will end up sabotaging your peace of mind. The thoughts, feelings, and beliefs we hold within in us create our reality, and so if you have heaviness or bitterness, or any other negative emotion weighing on your heart or cluttering your mind, you are telling yourself that you are choosing to live in the muck, and not where things are beautiful--so that is where your mind will take you, and that will become your reality. In doing this, you are essentially creating your own personal Hell within you. If you want to live on a higher level, you purposely need to move yourself to higher ground by choosing to have more positive, peaceful, compassionate thoughts.

As someone who has lived the life of an addict, chances are you are carrying around a lot of heavy baggage in your heart in the form of guilt, shame, remorse, and regret. You've seen and done things that you're not proud of, and moments and words loop around in your mind like a movie on replay. This is madness. You must create peace within yourself in order to heal. You must forgive yourself.

You're in luck though, because one thing that God is really good at is forgiveness. The split-second that a person realizes that they're sorry, or wishes they made a different choice in life, God is actually happy for you because within that pain you're feeling is a lesson learned, and God loves when we learn lessons! Just talk to God, and ask for his forgiveness and you will be forgiven instantaneously. If God can forgive you, you can most definitely forgive yourself. If you find yourself struggling with forgiving yourself, or forgiving others, I'd be happy to help you to work out any personal issues that may be holding you back from achieving inner peace.

You can't live in the present if you're always bringing up the past. You can't drive forward when you're too busy looking in the rearview mirror. The past is done and only exists in your mind… and you're the only one keeping it alive by reliving it over and over again. The question is, *why* do you want to keep it alive? *Why* can't you let it go? Is it because you feel like a victim? If so, please know that the people who hurt you throughout your life can try their best to victimize you, but it is *you*, and only *you*, who ultimately decides whether or not to step into the role of the victim and make it your identity. Forgiving people for what they ignorantly did to you takes their power and ability to control you away. It also causes your own personal power to increase, whereas feelings of anger, resentment, and defeat take your power away from you. Forgiveness literally makes you stronger because it removes any attachment to the event or person from your mind and your heart.

Forgiving others is very important to God because when we allow hate, fear, or anger into our lives, it stops the flow of love from God to ourselves, or from God, through us, to others, and when this happens God's will gets blocked by human stubbornness. This is a prime example of the freewill that God gives to us in action. He hopes that we'll always choose loving action, but if our human emotions control us, more than we control them, humans might wrongfully choose hate, over love.

You must remember, that when your life review comes, you will experience the hate, anger, and grudges you kept in your heart toward others as if you were on the receiving end of it yourself. You'll also get to experience the "ripple effect" that your stubbornness caused, because in life, our actions affect far more people than just ourselves and one other person. Forgive others and trust that God will one day show the person, or people who hurt you, how their actions made you feel. This is no longer your job. Turn it over to God and free yourself from the burden of it.

So what do I mean when I say "ripple effect"? Let's pretend for a moment that you are at your life review now, and a small insignificant moment in your life is revisited for you to experience. Let's say that you were driving in your car one day and some guy accidentally swerved into your lane almost hitting you. This made you very angry so you sped up, rolled down your window, and flipped him off while screaming out the window, "learn how to drive you idiot!" You're heated, but keep on driving and go on with your day, barely even remembering the incident by the end of the night. However, what happened to the person on the receiving end of your anger was a completely different story.

God then brings your perspective into the car with the person you flipped off. You are made to realize that he dropped a cigarette on his lap and it was burning him very badly and as he tried to brush it off, his car accidentally swerved into your lane. You see that he ended up with a permanent scar on his leg from it. When he got home he was still shaking from the incident and your voice was echoing in his head "learn how to drive you idiot!" He walks into his house to find that his young son is in a terrible mood because he had a bad day at school, and after trying to ignore his crying and screaming for a while, the man who cut you off screams at his son, "Shut up you idiot and stop crying." Staring at his Father in shock, the son felt frozen. You watch the boy and you are made to feel his young heart breaking inside from the realization that he must really be an idiot if his Father says he's an idiot.

So because of your anger and inability to forgive that person for simply being human and making a mistake, that child will end up believing for the rest of his life that he's an idiot. This belief ultimately causes the child not to try as hard throughout his life as he would have if he believed more in himself, which in turn makes him bitter and angry toward the world. He feels like a loser and therefore has trouble opening up to people and struggles with relationships. Then one day, he too calls his daughter an idiot and the cycle continues. This is an example of how God's love gets over-thrown when we don't live by the Divine Virtues. It's also an example of how powerful each and every one of us are and how impactful our words and actions are on the world we're living in. It's an example of how we're all connected and why it's so important to be mindful of our thoughts and actions, because these types of events happen behind the scenes all the time without people even realizing it.

Keep your heart open at all times to give God's love to others and to yourself through forgiveness. No matter what the situation may be. To forgive doesn't mean that you think what a person did was acceptable, justified, or right, it just means that you're not willing to lower your vibrational energy over some irrelevant human drama… and pretty much everything besides God's love is irrelevant in this world. When we die and go to Heaven, the only thing we will be judged on is how much we loved.

TWO: COURAGE

Courage is the possessing of the mental or moral strength to venture, persevere, or withstand danger, fear, difficulty, or grief.

Overcoming addiction, staying sober, and creating a life you love will most likely be the most courageous thing you do in your lifetime. Think about that. Isn't that incredible? At this very moment, you are being presented with the most momentous opportunity of your lifetime!

If your soul chose to experience addiction because it knew you needed to learn as many lessons in this one particular lifetime as was humanly possible, then this moment is exactly what your soul has been waiting for its entire life! Literally. Don't let yourself down now, be courageous and view this as a chance to get all of your lessons right this time. Stay courageous in your pursuit of information and knowledge. The fact that you're reading this book right now tells me that you are on the right path!

However, there is one way that you might end up sabotaging this opportunity and other opportunities in your lifetime if you're not careful, and that is by making excuses out of fear for why you simply cannot find the courage you need to have in order to achieve whatever it is that you want to accomplish.

It takes courage to change your life and it takes an incredible amount of strength to be courageous. It takes courage to trust your own convictions about what you want and what you don't want in life. It take courage to stand firm in your beliefs about what's right and wrong, good and bad, and to not be tempted to bend to what others might expect of you or hope you will do or think.

If you seek your strength internally from God, you will find the courage you need to make the changes you desire in your life. Even though trying to make permanent changes in your life may seem intimidating, rest assured that the hardest part of your journey is already over, because living in active addiction is more challenging than any self-improvement work you'll ever have to do.

Fear is the number one reason why humans stay stuck in their lives. Fear reveals itself in many different ways, but it's all created by the same defense mechanism within our minds known as the ego. I'll get more into the ego and how it operates a little later so that we can better understand it, but for now I want you to know that it is possible to override fear and that working on strengthening your courage will help you to do it. If you feel that you need help finding strength and courage, I'd be happy to help you discover it by working together to determine where your fearful hang-ups are coming from.

THREE: HUMILITY

Humility is the modest view of one's own importance in the world, acknowledging that you are just one small person in a world full of people. It's the realization that because of this, the world does not revolve around you. It's about continually considering the needs and feelings of others, not just your own. It also means that you are open to admitting when you are wrong or may not have the answers.

Being humble opens up doors for you to work closely with other people who may have the answers that you are seeking to have in your life. If your pride (otherwise known as your ego) gets in the way of who you really are, then you'll never find the answers that your true self, (your soul) is seeking because you'll be too proud to consider any other perspective or opinion besides your own.

Pride gets in the way of being able to keep an honest view of the truth within you. Living with an inflated ego will not serve you, it will only create a world of illusion for you to hide behind. If you are living a lie within yourself, you are only going to get false truths as a result of your inward reflection, and you'll be wasting your own time. When you are courageous enough to be honest, vulnerable, and communicate your insecurities and fears with someone who can help you, your world will begin to change for the better. As the saying goes "the truth shall set you free."

While I believe that we are all very special, and have our own unique gifts that God gives us to share with the world, flaunting those gifts in an effort to make ourselves feel like we are better than others is a quick way to show God that you are not responsible enough to handle those gifts, because in walking around acting like you're better than others, you are inadvertently making others feel less than, and that's not how to extend God's love to others. Part of humility is maintaining a quiet confidence when you could otherwise make a big deal out of yourself.

Trying to be bigger, louder, or cooler than your true self at base level, will prevent you achieving a connection with your higher self. Humility is understanding that you don't need to be more than who your soul is naturally in order to be enough. Our stories make us who we are, and that makes you special and unique just the way you are. All of this being said, you've been through so much and have come so far, so it's definitely okay to be proud of yourself and appreciate how far you've come.

FOUR: HONESTY

Honesty is the commitment to maintaining a truthful, honorable adherence to the facts without allowing your emotions, fears, or desires to influence you.

Honesty is about honoring God enough to not twist the current reality to suit your own needs and wants. When you manipulate the truth through lies, even the seemingly small lies you tell yourself, you get in the way of God's plan for you and for others. When this happens you actually end up delaying the good things that God has in store for you because a mistruth becomes a roadblock within your mind and heart which causes you to harbor a great many negative emotions and beliefs that end up altering your perception of reality. When your perception of reality is operating at a low, negative vibration, you are not operating as your higher self. Like attracts like, and therefore you cannot attract goodness with evil, or light with darkness.

Now, while all lies are not inherently evil, the devil is able to do his dirty work while hiding in the lies we tell ourselves and others, so please, if you love God, and you love yourself, do your best to never tell another lie ever again, no matter how insignificant it may seem at the time.

Be honest with yourself. If you are hurt, talk about the hurt. If you are angry, talk about the anger--don't try to heal yourself or get revenge on others by doctoring up a lie to make the truth hurt less. It's important to feel your feelings without lying to yourself about how you're actually feeling inside. There is so much knowledge to be gained and so many lessons to be learned from the truth, so why would you ever want to take that away from yourself?

The trap of delusion is the sneakiest form of dishonesty that humans can fall into. This is when people don't even realize that they are telling or crafting a mistruth and therefore end up believing their own lies. Sometimes people want so badly to believe their own lies because their lies lessen the pain they feel about the actual truth. Sometimes they do it to gain sympathy or attention. I cannot tell you how dangerous and toxic this could be to your life. I cannot begin to tell you how destructive delusion is to the human soul, and I beg you to realize that if any part of you is aware that you're lying to yourself or others about something, you should decide to do a complete 180 right at this very moment and transform your life by admitting the truth about yourself to yourself or to others. The next step is to find someone who can help you work through the healing related to your newfound honesty. I am here for you if you feel you need to work on being more honest with yourself.

Being honest about how you feel about yourself, your past, who you'd like to become, what your greatest challenges are, who has hurt you, and how they have hurt you, what you wish you had more of, or less of in your life, who you might have hurt, who you love, who you miss, who you hate… all of this needs to be released from your mind and from your heart. Once you bring it out of yourself into the world, you will be able to make your peace with all of it and it will feel absolutely incredible.

Over time, doing the heavy lifting of practicing complete honesty will strengthen your soul in so many ways that you will come to appreciate.

When you are no longer afraid of who you are, what your past was, and what others might think, that is when you will possess true freedom of spirit; but none of that will ever happen for you unless you are completely honest with yourself, and honest and sincere in your actions with others.

Integrity is the name of the game. Integrity is doing what is right, even when no one is watching. It's about possessing a character so strong that you know you can trust yourself with anything and somehow even strangers understand it too because you radiate a deeply honest energy; never judging others, never stealing, never deceiving, never manipulating, never gossiping, never using your words or actions in any way to hurt yourself or others. Never making drama where there doesn't need to be any. Living an honorable and honest life like this is a big responsibility that requires practice and dedication, but one that God needs for you to embrace in order to evolve your soul to the next level.

Love is the only universal truth, so when you feel frustrated, simply remind yourself to return to love in your heart, and let God inspire your thoughts and actions.

FIVE: FAITH

Faith is the road on which hope travels, and hope is the key to being able to possess optimism or optimistic thoughts that make the challenging times easier. Without hope, a person's soul becomes blind to the possibilities of a better future and when that happens, a person can only envision darkness, and you cannot be a mirror for God's light when you are living in the dark.

Faith comes from that little spark that's still left in your heart. No matter how tiny that spark might be, it can still be used to ignite a larger fire within you. Knowledge is like gasoline, the more you learn about God and yourself, the larger the fire will grow within you.

Faith is having complete confidence and trust in God's plan even when you don't understand it. Even when you feel tired, confused, and overwhelmed, lean back and hand over your stresses and anxieties to God. Say to Him, "I don't understand your plan, but I trust you. Please help me to... (state your requests of Him here)." Then, after you hand your concerns and stresses over to Him, you must let them go.

When you are praying to God, be sure to ask Him to show you how *you* can improve in order to fix the situation, and don't pray for other people to change to suit your needs. That's a total waste of time! The only thing we can control in this world is our ability to control ourselves, our outlook on things, and how we view the challenging situations in our life. Of course you can always pray that the other person receives the support from God they need in order to make a healthy, positive change in their life. Heartfelt, compassionate prayer for others is always viewed as another way to extend love to others.

For example, if you feel that life is caving in all around you, don't pray to God to make your challenges disappear, ask Him to make you stronger and wiser in order to handle them and sort through them more effectively. Or if someone is really bothering you, don't pray for them to go away, pray for the patience you need to deal with them. You must pray from a proactive, empowered perspective and not from a victim perspective. You'll never get the answers you seek, until you begin to step into your power and become the boss of your own life. In order to be the boss of your own life, you must not rely on anyone else besides yourself and God to fix your problems. Sure others can help you along the way, but continually playing the role of the victim in your life and always being in "pity party" mode will never serve you, and you'll never become the person you want to become if you are always hoping to receive sympathy from others. I promise you, once you shift your mindset to one of personal responsibility, assertiveness, and growth and start praying for God to help you become a better version of yourself, one trait at a time, your life will change drastically and so will your relationship with God and the people around you.

Once you pray for strength, your next step is to expect without a doubt to become stronger because God hears you, and if you ask for something that is going to help to grow your soul, the answer will always be yes! Sometimes when I pray for these things, I get the answers I'm seeking immediately. As if a wave of strength and peace has just washed over me. It's a beautiful feeling. Other times, answers don't come for days, months, or even years.

God knows when you are fully trusting Him, and when you are not, and the more faith you have, the more God knows you trust Him, and when He knows you trust Him, you become an unstoppable team. Things get much easier and synchronicities and "coincidences" related to what you prayed for, begin to happen a lot more often. When you have faith it's like stepping out of God's way as if to say "Do your thing God. I'm just going to step back and wait for the answer. I know you got me, just help me to be patient while I wait for the answer."

While you wait for the answer from God, be sure to quietly and calmly (while still trusting God to provide) search your soul for the voice within that will provide you with the answer. This voice is your higher consciousness, and it's the voice of your higher self which is your direct connection to God. Often your answers will feel like they are coming from within.

We all have two voices in our heads. One is the ego; it tries to keep us closed minded, small, scared, and weak. The other voice is our higher self; it wants us to grow, thrive, and find our strength. It hears what the ego says, but knows better than to listen to it. This is the voice you need to begin listening to. This voice is your best friend in life because this is the voice of God. It knows what is best for you, and the more you listen to it, the louder it will get until you'll eventually gain enough strength to drown out the voice of the ego and shut it down when you begin to sense that it's up to its old evil, manipulative tricks again. The voice of your higher self always knows what's best for you and will never steer you wrong. This voice is the key to possessing divine clarity. For the record, this voice will never tell you things that will hurt others or yourself. It will never create false realities. It will never choose evil and darkness over love and light. ALWAYS side with this voice, and stop letting your ego bring you back down to the dark side. DISCLAIMER: If you ever hear voices that encourage you to hurt yourself or others, that is not the voice of God, your Spirit Guides, Angels, or your higher self and they must be asked to leave permanently. If this is the case, please seek the guidance of a trained psychiatrist in your area who can help you. You should not try to manage a situation like this on your own. In life we must remember to remain open to seeking and receiving the help we need from others in order to thrive.

Just remember, God does not work on your timeline, he works on His, and on the timeline your soul needs to travel on in order for it to grow. When things get hard, you must ask yourself "what is this hardship trying to teach me?" Until you can answer that question while being very honest about how you could improve as a person, the hardships will persist. Just remember that God doesn't give us what we want, but He always gives us exactly what we need. It's up to us to figure out what hidden gifts, or lessons, the moments in our life are trying to provide us with. This way of thinking is a way of life in itself. It's a growth mindset that will make you incredibly knowledgeable.

Just a heads up; your ego will try to stop you from doing this type of inward reflection because it doesn't want you to feel the pain of being imperfect, but if you let your ego's voice win, then you are sabotaging yourself and your life. Throughout our lives we are in a constant battle with our own egos. Over time however, your ego will grow more and more quiet as it begins to realize that your higher self is the one in charge.

As you nurture the growth of your higher self by becoming smarter than your ego, like a lighthouse in a sea of darkness, the voice of God will become a powerful guiding light within your heart that will protect, strengthen, heal, and comfort you throughout your entire life. This is what it means to have a mindful heart. It's the ultimate goal, and the ultimate gift, because within this gift you will find yourself, and you will no longer feel lost at sea.

SIX: PATIENCE

Patience is the ability to tolerate or accept trouble, misfortune, pain, delay, or suffering without getting upset, losing your temper, complaining, becoming irritated, or annoyed.

You know the saying "patience is a virtue" well, it most certainly is because patience is a very challenging virtue to master. Patience is the ability to not let outside influences like people or situations, or inner influences like your ego or emotions, alter your inner peace.

We live in a world where we're constantly receiving input through our senses; sight, hearing, touch, sound, and taste. Sometimes these influences overstimulate or challenge one or more of our senses and we end up losing our cool or end up giving up on a goal we have set for ourselves because it challenges our internal ego.

Other people often challenge our egos through their words and actions and we become angry and lash out defensively towards them. There are many different ways a person can become triggered and therefore impatient.

When we lose control of our centeredness, we lose control of ourselves. To combat this we have to learn to protect ourselves by becoming unshakable by the human world and our own egos. The trick is to tame the ego, so that you don't take offense to the feedback others are giving you in the first place. First off, you have to understand that each person in the world is operating on a different level based on the knowledge they possess. So one person's opinion of you should not be viewed or interpreted as an accurate reflection of your own self-worth. That person is not qualified to do that. The only judge of yourself, should be yourself, because you are the only one who fully understands your entire life journey and the intentions behind your past actions. The only thing you should judge yourself on is how hard you are trying to evolve and how closely you are living your life as a mirror of God's love back to yourself, others, and the world around you.

The ego's need for approval, praise, and acceptance makes us upset when those needs are challenged or not met. In the moments when we find ourselves getting upset over something someone said, or did, pause before reacting and remember to respond back lovingly and patiently, even if the person was out of line.

While forming your response, you must remember that this person does not have all the information they need to form a correct opinion about you, so their opinions are not entirely accurate. You must remember that because they are only human too, they are also dealing with their own egos that may be blindly judging you without a healthy motive behind it besides their own need to feel superior to you. (The ego always wants to feel special and superior.) So while forming your response, be patient with the other person for simply being human just like you.

God is incredibly patient with us. He understands that we are all struggling on this human journey to figure everything out. He understands that we're going to mess up and he has nothing but compassion for us when we do. He's even proud of us even when we fail because that means that we were bold enough to try and change for the better.

Besides becoming impatient with others, humans have a tendency to be very impatient with themselves and their own progress. We want fast results and feel intimidated by things that require a long time commitment to master, but the often slow process of learning and growing in life *is* the whole point of life and it can't be rushed. In fact, it should be appreciated and enjoyed for exactly what it is; a never ending, transformative evolution that is messy, disruptive, shocking, and eye opening. Many things in a person's life need to fall apart so that the pieces can come together in a divinely beautiful new way, and that is not a delicate process. Remember to be your own best friend and be patient with yourself throughout this extraordinary journey called life. Don't expect perfection. That's too much pressure to put on yourself.

The only things we can control in life are our own thoughts and actions. When we feel ourselves starting to get angry or annoyed, or when we start to feel defeated, this is a great opportunity for learning. Why are we getting angry? Why are we so annoyed by this? Why are we feeling defeated? If you stay honest with yourself, and keep breaking your emotions down layer by layer, eventually you'll get to the truth and you will free yourself of that negative emotion... as long as you're patient enough to do it.

SEVEN: SIMPLICITY

Simplicity is the quality or condition of being uncomplicated, natural, effortless, straightforward, and unpretentious.

Simplicity, when integrated into a person's life, works wonders to relieve anxiety, confusion, and the illusion and stress of trying to be someone you are not. Simple is real and real is honest.

Simplicity is the ultimate goal. This is where everything in your life is uncluttered and uncomplicated, including your mind, your spirit, and even your physical home.

Refusing to do the work to live an uncomplicated life will bite you in the butt every single time because it is not your higher self that complicates things; it's your ever annoying ego at play, and when ego is involved you will always end up sabotaging even your best intentioned personal growth efforts.

When you learn how to lead a simple life there will be no drama, no gossip, no grudges, no jealousy, no competing against others, no judgement, and no manipulation of people or situations to suit your own needs. Sounds like a beautiful and peaceful way to live don't you think?

The ego though, likes to create drama so that you can feel like the hero or the victim. It likes to gossip to make you feel superior, or attacked in order to receive sympathy from others. It likes to hold grudges to show others how powerful you are. It's jealous of others because it fears not being good enough as you are. The list goes on. When it comes to creating a life you love, you need to do your best to let go of your attachment to your ego once and for all because your ego is not your friend.

Once your ego has shrunk, it will be easier for you to accept yourself and others. You'll become less anxious, less depressed, more peaceful, more optimistic, and more courageous.

To simplify your life, you need to know in your heart that you don't need much more than a roof over your head, clothing on your back, food in your belly, and love, to be happy and satisfied. There is so much love around you and so many people that care about you, even if those people might be strangers. Love is the energy of God's Universe and it connects us all.

God is a very simple being. Some people who have had a near death experience recall that when the meaning of life was revealed to them, they were astonished to learn that it was all so simple that a child could understand it. Let's keep that in mind when trying to build and create our own lives. If God can create an entire planet with billions of people on it, and manage to make the meaning of life simple, surely we can do it too within our own lives. When life gets complicated, keep it simple and always return to love.

I used to work in marketing. I gave that career up because I realized it was my calling to help people learn to love themselves, their lives, and each other. Even though I went to school for marketing and sunk a ton of money into a degree, I just couldn't stomach the industry anymore. For the most part, marketing and advertising tries to manipulate people into feeling like they need to buy a specific thing in order to fill an unnamable void inside of them. Let's be honest, there's not one single material item that you can purchase on this planet that will fill the void you are looking to fill in your heart. The only thing that can fill that is love and God. End of discussion. That being said, doesn't that make your life so much more simple right out of the gate, knowing that you can stop buying stuff you don't need now because it's never going to give you the results you want anyhow?

Declutter your mind by learning the difference between a need and a want. Don't fall prey to the marketing that you are bombarded with every single day on social media, television, and in magazines. See it for what it is, the attempt to keep you forever searching for your joy though material possessions and products just so businesses can make a profit from you. This is a toxic way to live, continually trying to consume your way to happiness. The more you want, the less happy you'll be, because one person can never have it all. If you learn to be happier with less, then you'll always have more than you need.

When it comes to relationships, simplicity can be tricky. Some people in our lives make us feel good. We enjoy their company and they enjoy ours. Others challenge us, but we know they mean well or just don't know any better. Then there are people in our lives who are toxic and continually bring us down and disrupt our peace of mind.

While holding frivolous grudges only complicates things and they are not worth engaging in, there are rare occasions in life where boundaries need to be drawn, and people need to be removed from your life in the most peaceful way possible in order to protect yourself and your sanity.

This is especially true when the people in your life are other addicts that continually remind you of your past and make you feel weak. You find their presence comforting because they are people you know and love, but by simply being in their presence, part of you feels the urge to use again. The lousy thing about a relationship like this is that your sobriety doesn't just depend on your own willpower, it also depends on theirs, and that's a dangerous situation to put yourself in.

You must look out for yourself in situations like this and do what you need to do to simplify your life and calm your mind. This is going to require that you peacefully separate from the bad influences in your life. At least until you are many years sober and can safely hang out again. It doesn't need to be forever, but it does need to happen, and it needs to happen before you slip up and end up regretting it. This is your opportunity to prevent a future self-sabotaging moment.

One way to do this is to write them a letter where you let them know what your goals are for yourself, and that you need to do all you can to make sure you pave that road for yourself to travel down. Tell them that you love them, and that you want the best in the world for them, but that for now, you have to cut the ties that keep you bound to your past. A past that you're trying to move on from. If they really love you, they will set you free. Their ego may take a blow, and it may hurt them, and they may try to fight it or get angry, but you have to know that their love for you without the influence of ego, only wants what's best for you, so you have to tell yourself that they really do want you to be happy, they just don't know how to say goodbye.

Life is bittersweet at times, but the show must go on. Appreciate the poetic nature of the moment for the dramatic energy it holds knowing in your heart that you are going to be successful because you were brave enough to choose YOU!

EIGHT: GRATITUDE

Gratitude is the ability to feel appreciation for the things and people in your life that make your life better.

If a person lives their life without enough gratitude in their heart, they will always feel as if other people have more than they do, and that *they* are somehow being cheated out of not having enough in life. A person who believes these lies will eventually assume a victim mentality in their minds, and therefore that is the filter they will view and process the world through, and through this filter, the world looks very unfair. How can a person find happiness if they feel the world is failing them?

People who go through life playing the victim role exude a sort of desperation that other people pick up on very easily. They become takers instead of givers because they feel the world owes them something, but what does that mean for the people that are being taken from? How is that any more fair? It's not, but takers don't care.

Living life as this type of person is the quickest way to sabotage your own happiness and genuine relationships with others. So let's make sure that doesn't happen to you.

When God made the Earth He made it plentiful so that there would always be enough for everyone as long as long as they remained simple and did not become greedy. First world humans have lost touch with what it means to have "enough" though. We've gotten away from basics and have come to expect a lot more, all of the time. New, bigger, better, faster is the name of the game these days.

Now you may have noticed, that this is where the lines of simplicity begin to run into gratitude. Life is not about having more, it's about becoming happier with less. If you focus on what you do have in your life, vs what you don't have, you'll always have enough. Gratitude turns not enough, into enough, and when a person feels that they have enough in their life, they can finally view themselves as fortunate, lucky, and blessed.

The best way to start, is to start small. Give thanks to God for the clothes on your back, the food you ate today, the roof over your head, the running water in your home, the bed you are sleeping in. Make a commitment to yourself that for the next week you will focus on giving thanks to God for the small and simple things all around you that you never before paid much attention to.

For example, one night while out to dinner with my family, I excused myself to use the bathroom. I was feeling a heavy burden within me that night and I just couldn't tell why I was feeling so unhappy. As I stood there gazing sadly at myself in the mirror, I reached down to put soap on my hands. To my surprise, when the soap came out it was foamy and not the gel kind. (This is when foamy soap was new on the public restroom scene). I stared at the blossom of soap in my hand and I decided right then and there, that from now on, I was going to start to find my happiness in even the smallest of things. Like foamy soap.

Making radical gratitude a habit in my daily routine has made me more aware of the little things around me which bring me joy, such as how the sunlight dances off the wall in the mornings, how my husband looks at my daughter with such adoring love in his eyes, how the mail person does such a good job at delivering our packages dependably each day, the smell of fresh cut grass, or even the smell of my stinky bulldog Otis. No longer do I feel the need to go shopping for random "stuff" to try and fill a mysterious void within me, which is something I used to do quite a bit. Gratitude has filled that void for me and I have learned that the little things *are* the big things in life.

When you spend your days being thankful for all of the elements that make up your life, like the everyday moments, other people, the lessons, the sights, the sounds, the smells, the tastes, and the touches, your world will become so rich and abundant that you will praise God every day for being lucky enough to be alive and sober to experience it all.

Another thing you have to be grateful for are the traumas you have been through in your life. The challenging times that have forced you to evolve as a person. The moments that leave a mark on your soul to remind you how far you've come. Be sure to acknowledge and give thanks for the challenging experiences that helped to form you into who you are. Love the moments for the knowledge they have provided you with. At the same time, be sure not to cling so tightly to your past traumas that they become your identity. While honoring these experiences, don't allow them to keep you tied to the past out of fear of moving forward into the unknown future.

Life is not supposed to be perfect or easy because life is for learning and growing. It's messy and complicated and that's okay. Anyone who pretends to be perfect, or who thinks that their traumas should be discarded, isn't fully accepting themselves and honoring their own unique story. Be proud of who you are, what you've been through and all that you've overcome. Loving your own unique journey is your super power because when you do that you'll finally be able to accept and love yourself just as you are.

When people realize just how fortunate they are to be a part of this crazy thing called life, it often makes them feel as if their cup is overflowing with goodness, so much so, that they feel the need to share it with others. The best way to give thanks and show your gratitude for the gift of life is to be generous in the giving of yourself to other people in the world.

Generosity is the act of giving to or serving others from your heart out of love. This could be giving of your time, your attention, your money, or your talents, but whichever way you choose to show your generosity towards others, you must do so with the best intentions in your heart. For example, there are many people who donate to charities simply for the tax deduction, and in God's eyes, their giving is being done for personal gain and not to help others. God always understands our true intentions.

When we serve others out of love, our life becomes meaningful and full of purpose. If we were the only person on the planet, who we hope to become in our life would forever remain a figment of our imagination. That's because we discover ourselves through others, and there's no greater feeling in the world than realizing that because of you, someone else on this planet is breathing a little easier and smiling a little brighter. This is what it means to be a mirror of God's unconditional love.

Before we can do that though, we must first learn how to accept and love ourselves, flaws and all. It is then that we can openly share that love with others and truly feel connected to the energy of God's unconditional love that runs like a network over, around, and through the entire Universe from person to person, atom to atom. Love is the energy that binds us all as one and it feels incredibly empowering and peaceful to be a part of that oneness.

CHAPTER 7

LESSON 4:
MODALITIES OF
MINDFUL THINKING

Strengthening your spirituality and learning to trust and turn to God in times of pain, stress, and confusion can solve so many problems for you, but there's something else that sabotages people time and time again, and that is how they process and interpret the world around them.

I've mentioned a few times throughout the book that our thoughts form our reality, so therefore we need to be very mindful about *how* information gets processed as it enters our minds.

As we go about our daily lives, we are constantly evaluating and forming opinions about the world around us. This is a normal function of the human brain which has made it possible for the human species to survive for thousands and thousands of years by helping us to avoid dangerous situations and people that may cause us harm or death.

However there's another side to this function that can be very dangerous for humans in the long run, and that is when we trust our immediate thoughts too much and never question the feelings, beliefs, and attitudes within us that worked to form that thought.

Feelings are fleeting. One day we feel on top of the world, the next you might feel down in the dumps. If the quality of your life is based on how you are feeling from moment-to-moment, you are going to live a very unstable life. Remember, just because you are feeling something, doesn't make it true or absolute.

You see, the only way to live a life free of the torture of your own inconstant mind, is to live completely in truth, and truth is not possible when a person lives within the confining walls of their own set perceptions that they have learned about the world that were built out of fear and ego.

We cannot evolve when we cling to ideas about ourselves and the world that we developed when we were young. Genuine maturity takes place when a person decides to become a life-long student of truth, and is willing to take personal responsibility for managing their own thoughts and feelings within the truth. Once a person masters this skill, everything in their life becomes possible and achievable.

The good news is that our brains are flexible and no matter how old we are, we are always able to change patterns of thinking that no longer serve us. Our brains possess something called neuroplasticity, and this allows our brains to rewire themselves in response to new learning experiences.

Now let's uncover exactly what this "truth" is that I'm speaking of by taking a look at 4 Mindful Modalities. Most people view the world in relation to themselves, but with only one of you in the world, and billions of other people, this narrow-minded way of perceiving the world doesn't take anything or anyone else into consideration except one's own existence. As we discussed earlier, we cannot possibly realize our own greatness without directly inter-acting with other people, so taking on a self-centered view of the world will not serve you well in life. Being able to view the world, others, and even yourself outside of your own emotions is the pathway to true enlightenment.

I want to teach you how to change the way you process the world around you, so that you have the power to control your emotions. In learning how to do this, your emotions can no longer hold you captive. Let's break it down.

ONE: INTERPRETATION

When any kind of event or situation comes up in a per-son's life, this is called an "External Event." This could be anything from someone stealing your parking spot, to the guilt you feel about a bad decision you made. An External Event is anything that happens to you in life at any time.

When an External Event enters your mind through your senses, this is where the journey of information begins within you, and this is where you can choose to do one of two things. One: You can choose to default to your same old way of thinking (or not thinking at all) and let your emo-tions determine the outcome and therefore your future, or TWO: You can step into your power as a critically thinking human with a higher level of consciousness by choosing how you think and respond toward yourself and others.

By choosing number two, you are intentionally choosing to live life as your higher self and create your own reality by mindfully managing your thoughts.

As an External Event enters your brain, it immediately begins to pass through a variety of filters that have been created in your mind throughout your life; filters such as your beliefs, values, and memories. External Events also pass through filters such as Generalizations, Deletions and Distortions which are all elements of "distorted thinking," which we'll get into in just a moment.

Beliefs are what you have come to believe about a certain thing or person through the experiences and memories you have had in your life, or through the influence of what other people have taught you to believe about a certain thing or person.

Beliefs are always limited in nature because there's no way that a person can know everything. So right away, an enlightened person understands that they're never operating with all of the facts to make an observation that is completely founded in truth.

Values are what make up your moral compass and the 8 Divine Virtues that we studied in the last chapter are a major part of those values.

Generalization is a mode of distorted thinking that people often engage in that casts a blanket of false judgement over a large group of people or things based on just a few opinions. Generalizations such as "*all* therapists are quacks." Generalizations are often made against things such as careers, religions, skin color, sexual orientation, race, or gender and even against addicts. Generalizations create lies about people and things, which in turn limits our potential for growth by keeping our minds closed off to the potential of the world. The one who ends up being hurt the most by a generalization, is the person who believes it. If you are committed to living in truth, you will not jump to conclusions and believe the mistruths that blanket generalizations create.

What a terrible thing it would be if God generalized all humans and believed that "all humans were terrible people" and therefore wanted nothing to do with us. What if the actions of a few bad people caused all of humanity to suffer and miss out on God's comfort and love?

Thankfully for us, God is far too enlightened to ever do this. God views each one of us as an individual soul, and each one of us is very special, unique, and important in His eyes. If it is your goal to live in truth, and be the light of God throughout your life, you will do all you can to love each person you meet in life as an individual soul worthy of the same love and compassion that you also deserve.

Approach all people with an open mind that holds no preconceived notions about how they are going to be or treat you. Doing away with this habit of toxic thinking will create so many opportunities in life for you, and it will help you to feel more connected to all of humanity and less afraid. It will also do the same for the people on the receiving end of your prior false judgements. It's a win, win.

Of course, if you meet someone and your gut tells you that you are in danger, please always listen to that instinct. Never override your survival-based gut instincts. God gave us that gift for a reason, just be sure that your preconceived beliefs are not wrongfully influencing your judgements.

Next on the list of distorted thinking are "Deletions." Deletions are when we conveniently delete from our minds the role that we have played in hurting other people. Unfortunately, no matter how hard we try, we will never be able to fully understand how our words and actions have effected people, simply because we are not them. Their pain is not memorable to us because we have not been directly affected by it.

Many people get defensive when others tell them how they have been hurt or disappointed, but this is mostly because our ego doesn't want to admit that we are an imperfect human being who sometimes makes mistakes.

The best way to combat this toxic way of thinking is to strengthen your empathy skills. First off, you must realize that people are allowed to feel any way they want to feel regardless of your intention. Even if you didn't mean to hurt someone, but they still ended up hurt, you need to respect that and use it as an opportunity to learn more about yourself. You cannot control how other people feel, you can only control your response to it.

If you are unsure how you hurt someone, ask questions until you understand better. Even if you don't agree, listen patiently without taking it too personally. If you look at the conversation as a blessing and opportunity to grow your awareness, you'll view it with a positive twist on it, which will help to ease your own ego's disappointment, hurt, and anger. Even if you don't understand how the person could be so hurt, respond with compassion and offer a genuine apology if you feel it would make the person feel better, or continue the conversation with patience and a genuine desire to reach common ground.

Approaching life with a desire to make others feel seen, comfortable, respected, and appreciated while in your presence is a beautiful way to spread God's love. Here's a warning though, this shouldn't be done to the point where you become a people pleaser and get taken advantage of by the "takers" in this world. You never want to give so much that you become a doormat and lose yourself in the process. If you feel that this is happening, you must set reasonable boundaries to protect yourself.

The final filter is called "Distortions." This is when humans jump to drastic, inaccurate conclusions quickly without much information, thought, or reason. This toxic, and self-sabotaging way of thinking, often reveals itself through worst case scenario thinking, or all or nothing thinking, both of which do not live in reality.

With worst case scenario thinking, a person has already determined in their mind that a negative result is the only result they could possibly end up with, and therefore that's usually what they'll get.

A self-fulfilling prophecy is when a person unknowingly causes a prediction to come true, due to the simple fact that they expect it to come true. Our brains are very powerful, and our thoughts, belief system, and how we view the world truly do create our reality. We must be very careful to be mindful of the thoughts we think, because one way or another, they'll end up working for us, or against us. You can create a beautiful new life for yourself simply by being mindful about the thoughts you choose to think.

And last, but not least, with all or nothing thinking, a person stubbornly rejects any version of an outcome other than the one that they most desire, with zero room for flexibility or compromise. This way of thinking stops people from gracefully accepting God's plan for them and they end up resisting their own destiny instead of being open to discovering it.

TWO: PERCEPTION

Now that you understand more about interpretation and the filters which External Events pass through when they first reach our brains, the next step in the processing of an External Event is called "Perception." Perception is when our brains take the newly interpreted information, and attach a personal meaning to it.

When this new information makes its way through our brains, the first thing the brain tries to do is understand how to interpret it. This seemingly insignificant moment is where so many people end up sabotaging their happiness. This is where we assign a personal story to the information and determine how this information will forever become a part of us.

For example, let's say that you were at work and completely messed up a major project that is due tomorrow. Your boss has made it very clear that he is upset with you. This is where your brain will begin to assign a meaning to the External Event of your boss being mad at you and the botched project.

If a person isn't mindful of the thoughts they think, they might say something to themselves like, "I'm so stupid. How could I be so careless? I must be an idiot to mess something like this up." This type of negative self-talk is toxic and will eventually cause you not to trust yourself to manage anything in your own life properly, and as we discussed a few paragraphs ago, these types of thoughts become self-fulfilling prophecies that will come true simply because you believe them, and will end up sabotaging your success.

Now that you've made this your reality, you'll continue through life feeling that you can never do anything right, and the cycle of being proved right time and time again will persist until you step up and intentionally decide to silence the bully within your brain by taking steps to improve the way you speak to yourself.

Our inner-monologue is the voice within us that we choose to speak to ourselves in. It can be positive or negative and therefore either work for us, or against us.

As I mentioned earlier, there are two voices within us that we can choose to listen to. One is our ego, which operates out of fear and tries to keep us small and weak, and therefore "safe" so that we never get hurt by trying and failing again. (The ego's reasoning is very weird.) The other is the voice of our higher self which operates out of love, forgiveness, and encouragement and the understanding that we are only human and make mistakes.

If you were living as your higher self, your inner-monologue might go something like this instead, "Oh man, I really messed that up, but by failing I now understand exactly what my boss needs from me and now I'll never make that mistake again. I'm glad I got that out of the way because now I can really do a great job the next time. I'm going to work extra hard to make this up to my boss." This way of talking to yourself looks at the situation as simply a setback and not as proof that you are a failure. With this way of thinking, you will become more resilient and optimistic and will approach future projects with the belief that no matter what happens you will make the most out of it and will end up stronger and smarter than you were when the project began.

By this example, can you see how absolutely critical it is that you become vigilantly mindful about the meanings you assign to the events in your life? It's not the events in our life that end up hurting us, it's the stories we tell ourselves about the events in our life that end up hurting us, or helping us. The choice is yours!

If you come away with one thing after reading this book, I hope you will remember this lesson. How you think and speak to yourself creates your reality and determines how much you will be able to love and respect yourself throughout your life. Also, a person will never be able to give the love to others, which they don't first possess for themselves. A person can't pour from an empty cup, right?

If you've ever wondered why you can't seem to maintain healthy relationships with others, this is a big component of why. As cliché as it sounds, if you don't love yourself, you have no love to give, and therefore cannot share an honest, healthy love with others. When you don't have love for yourself, you end up looking to others to fill the void within you, and therefore, other people end up becoming the determining factor of your own self-worth and happiness, and that's a very dangerous place to be mentally and emotionally. Take the time to learn to love yourself and your life will change drastically.

THREE: INTENTION

We must be mindful that the stories we tell ourselves over and over again, eventually become our beliefs. This means that we are constantly, yet unconsciously, forming our own version of the truth all of the time. This can be a good thing when you choose to view the world through the lens of your higher self, living in God's love and light inspired by the Divine Virtues, but it can become a bad thing when you let your raw, unexamined emotions call the shots.

Not only does our inner-monologue determine how we feel about ourselves, it determines how we feel about others. For example, if there is a particular person in your life who annoys you, you can choose to keep the peace between the two of you by not feeding the ego side of you which wants to think and speak badly about them. As tempting as it may be, doing so destroys the truth, which is that we are all divine beings, souls that are learning and growing every single day. Who a person is today, may not be who they are tomorrow.

Assuming the worst about someone completely ruins your ability to view them in any other light besides the negative one that you have created, and this ultimately ends up destroying relationships. When people do not live in harmony, there is a ripple effect which casts rings of negative energy out into the world instead of God's beautiful energy of unconditional love.

When this love is disrupted by human ignorance, we end up doing a major disservice to all of humanity, because God's uncomplicated loving energy has the ability to heal everything that it is allowed to touch. If your actions, thoughts, beliefs, assumptions, and values interrupt the flow of love, generosity, understanding, patience, and forgiveness while you are alive, you are not serving God, others, or yourself properly. When God's love is interrupted, people suffer and I don't know about you, but at the end of my life, I want to know that I brought love and light into this world, to the best of my ability.

When you recognize feelings that do not stem from love coming from your ego, being directed toward others or toward yourself, remind yourself that your spirit, or higher self, wants nothing to do with anything except what is good and right in God's eyes--so forgive others for being imperfect the same way you would want God to forgive you for being imperfect. Remember to hold space in your heart for others and yourself to grow and evolve a little more each day. This is why we are all here having this Earthly experience together--so that we can learn from one another.

Humans must be mindful to not engage in hypocritical thinking. For example, if Sara said or did something to another person that hurt them, chances are she'd expect that person to forgive her quickly without much upset. However, if someone said or did something to hurt Sara, her knee-jerk reaction would most likely be to get angry and not move toward forgiveness very quickly. Often this initial approach to hurt ends up with people holding onto childish grudges in order to try and punish the other person. In a truthful world, there cannot be two different measures of judgement. We must treat others how we wish to be treated at all times, even when it's not our first response.

When you live with peaceful intention, and master the loving art of forgiveness, the toxic habit of judgement will begin to disappear like magic, because when you live with pure forgiveness in your heart for everyone, you come to realize that it's okay to be imperfect. As an added bonus, embracing this understanding will help you to love, forgive, and accept your own self more and more each day, and that is the best gift you could ever give to yourself.

FOUR: RESPONSE

We must remember in all of this, that our initial perception of the world is not reality. It's whatever we make it out to be. Whatever we make it out to be becomes our emotional state and our emotional state determines how we respond to others. It's our job as enlightened souls to do our best, to make sure that our emotional state remains in alignment with our higher self so that we can respond to others with compassion and love.

We must make sure that the thoughts we think take us to where we want to be emotionally so that we can put out into the world the energy that will transform us into the people we most want to become. If you can master this process, you will have a beautiful life.

No one in this whole world can make you feel a certain way without your permission. The second you begin to feel hurt, be sure to step into the role of your higher self and choose to talk to yourself with the voice of compassion, support, and forgiveness.

When we respond to others in a way which proves that we are able to control our own emotions, we develop a newfound confidence in our abilities to control our entire lives, which leads to a big boost in our self-esteem that will keep growing stronger and stronger with each passing day.

CHAPTER 8

LESSON 5:
THE HONEST MIRROR

My favorite quote in the entire world is by Socrates—"The unexamined life is not worth living." This quote resonates deeply within me because I know that the reason we are all here is to learn more about ourselves and others. If we ignore examining our life because we're too afraid to feel things, then we're literally wasting our entire life by allowing fear to control us from the inside out.

I refuse to let fear rule my life, and I hope that you will join me in doing all you can to suck every last drop of knowledge out of your life experiences, because within each drop of knowledge is a chance at a better, more fulfilling, more content existence.

When we die there are two things that we are allowed to take with us, and that is the love we have for the people (and animals) in our lives, and the lessons we have learned which become a part of our soul's permanent wisdom. We also carry this wisdom into our future lifetimes so we don't have to repeat the lessons that once held us back. Because of this your future lives will become easier to manage because you'll have the skillset within you to deal with your challenges in a more effective and productive way. Friendly Disclaimer: This does not mean that your future lives will be a breeze because as I mentioned at the beginning of the book, we purposely choose our biggest life challenges based on the lessons our soul needs to learn within our upcoming lifetime. We do this because humans simply don't learn when things are easy. The pain we experience throughout life provides us with a profound understanding, not just knowledge. It's one thing to imagine what something might be like. It's another thing entirely to live it and experience it firsthand.

So what are the lessons you need to learn from your addiction? The only way to find out is to dive in and see what you can discover about yourself by being completely honest and vulnerable in your evaluation of yourself, what you've been through in your life, and how you view the world. Inward reflection doesn't need to be scary, or painful. When you approach it with love, compassion, understanding, and forgiveness towards yourself, and a respect for the process of learning and growing, it can actually become something that you get excited about and look forward to doing each day of your life! Out with the old, and in with the new.

When I learn something new about myself that I don't like, that I realize I need to improve upon, I feel as if I just received a gift from the Universe and an opportunity to advance my soul to the next level, therefore allowing me to become closer to God. I give thanks for the new insight and then commit to doing the work needed to make the change within myself. Maybe that's reading a book, or signing up for a program that I feel will help me.

Where to start is probably the most intimidating thing about beginning your journey toward enlightenment. To help you take the first steps in understanding more about yourself, I've put together a list of questions to ask yourself. Be sure to answer these questions as honestly and openly as possible.

Remember, there is no judgement, only growth. If you start to feel overwhelmed by the questions, return to love in your heart, and remember to forgive yourself for simply being human. Know that God, your Angels, and your Spirit Guides are watching over you and are proud of the person you are striving to become.

Are you embarrassed or shamed by your addiction? What is it exactly that embarrasses or shames you?

Is there anything else in your past, unrelated to your addiction, that you are embarrassed about or feel shameful about?

What kind of lessons do you think your addiction is trying to teach you? What do you feel you could improve upon based on what you've learned so far in this book?

What are your unmet needs? What do you want to be, do, and have in your life?

What excuses, or lies, have you been telling yourself about why you can't achieve your goals or have certain things in your life? What has that bullying voice inside your mind been telling you about yourself, that your higher self knows is untrue?

From what you've read in the book, how do you think you've been sabotaging yourself?

What is hurting you mentally, emotionally, physically?

What are you angry about?

What are you bitter about or what are you holding grudges about? Who is this destroying relationships with in your life?

Do you have unrealistic expectations about how things "should be" in life? Give examples of how you feel let down in life by unmet expectations.

What kind of negative repeating patterns or situations have you noticed in your life? This could be in the form of results you keep getting, or not getting. Repeating thoughts, actions, or words.

In your life do you feel that you are you mostly taking from people, or mostly giving to people? Why do you feel that way?

If you'd like for me to elaborate on any of these questions, send me a message through the contact form on my website so that I can better explain them to you.

Learning to trust God's plan for your soul is so important, because in doing so, you are finally free of the worries that once held you back. When you trust in God completely, and surrender your life and its plan over to Him, you won't feel the need to focus on anything else besides the sheer gift to grow that is being given to you.

Surrendering completely to God will conquer feelings of loneliness, fear, despair, and anxiety. You'll understand that God is always there for you, even when other humans might not be. There will be nothing to fear because God would never give you something that He didn't think you could handle, and you are never alone in your struggles. There will be no despair because you'll always know that there is a bigger plan underway, a plan which you might not understand, but that you respect and trust. There will be no more anxiety because there will no longer be any need for you to try and control something that you never had any control over in the first place. We are all living God's plan whether we realize it or not. The only difference is that some people resist it, and others go with the flow.

In surrendering completely to God you become like a sailboat that has just broken free from its burdensome anchor. Free for God to direct ever so gently with the wind. You are the Captain of your life and God is your north star. Communicate with God every day. Let Him know what you want, what you need help with, and where you need strength and he will adjust the wind in your sails accordingly, as long as this keeps you on your life's path and moving toward your destiny. Trust that even if you don't get what you want, you'll always get what you need.

As you learn what you need to learn, new doors will begin opening up for you that will lead you to new opportunities and experiences that are literally waiting for you right now. Waiting for you to enter into them as the new and improved upon you. This process is never-ending and will continue throughout your entire life, so never stop striving to become the next best version of yourself and the opportunities will never cease. You will be amazed at what happens when you are in alignment with your higher self and God. Miracles and synchronicities will begin to happen to you, and for you, more often than you can imagine.

CHAPTER 9

LESSON 6:
STRATEGIES FOR AVOIDING RELAPSE

There are two types of moments that you need to be prepared for when it comes to avoiding relapse. The times where you may feel the urge to use because you are experiencing some sort of emotion that makes you want to feel numb instead of feeling that particular emotion, and moments where your "drug of choice" is staring you straight in the face tempting you to use again.

In the moments when you are faced with feeling the urge to use again because you'd rather feel nothing, here are some thoughts to consider:

All your problems, no matter how much pain they may be causing you, are temporary. Don't let this temporary moment of sadness, anger, or disappointment destroy all you have worked so hard for. The only thing permanent in life is change. Even the good times are temporary, so if you allow yourself to fall to pieces every time things aren't great, then you're subconsciously giving yourself permission to numb the pain; and that mentality will eventually lead to relapsing. Life is not supposed to be perfect or easy, and the sooner a person can accept that, the less disappointing life will become.

Life is a rollercoaster ride of emotions that each and every one of us is on, and it's our job to steadily, calmly, and consistently hang on for the ride. There is no escape other than directly dealing with our emotions head on as they arise.

Enjoy the points of the ride when life is good and happy, and enjoy the times when life is calm and uneventful, and when the challenging times come along, do all you can to turn them into something positive by trying to discover the lessons that they are trying to teach you about yourself and the world.

If you're having a bad day, remind yourself that it's just a bad day, not a bad life, and that how you feel right now is only temporary. Spend the rest of the day taking care of yourself by doing things that bring you joy. Like taking a hot shower, or diffusing your favorite essential oils, burning a candle, journaling or reading or listening to your favorite music, drawing, yoga, meditating, or even taking a short nap or a walk in nature. In fact, spending time in nature, unplugged from our crazy digital world is a very effective way to energetically reconnect with God--the creator of everything--and to realign yourself.

Even if you don't necessarily feel like talking, when you're feeling overwhelmed, that's the perfect time to call a friend, mentor, or sponsor who lifts you up when you're feeling down.

People often end up relapsing when their emotions go unexamined for too long and accumulate to the point where they become overwhelming and unbearable. Many people don't even realize it's happening until it's too late, so it's really important to make introspection and self-care a part of your daily life.

There's another way to prevent your emotions from getting out of control, and that is to pay close attention to your body for signs that something is "off."

Have you ever noticed that when you experience an emotion, like anger for example, your stomach begins to feel acidic, or like it's twisted in knots, or like it's rumbling or shaking? Or perhaps your mind races with negative thoughts that seem to spiral out of control.

Or maybe when you're sad, you feel like you have a pit in your stomach, or that your heart feels heavy or hurts. Or perhaps your mind begins to bring you down into the sadness.

Your body is a powerful tool that can be used as an early warning system to keep your emotions from becoming unbearable. Tune into the language of your body by paying attention to the physical sensations you are feeling within your body and mind. Once you recognize something other than a level, calm, centered feeling, ask yourself if something happened recently to trigger that feeling. Was something said or done to you? Did you think a certain thought? Did you do something, or not do something, that is making you feel this way?

Be sure to treat your emotions with respect. You are not bad, or weird, or wrong for having them. You are a completely normal human. Instead of trying to push the bad feelings away, acknowledge them and greet them with an open mind, and an open heart. They are there trying to tell you something important. Our emotions are a gift. Be grateful for them, then do the work to decode the meaning and lessons within them.

View your emotions as a guest that stopped by for a quick visit. Some questions to ask your emotions are: "Why are you here?" "What's wrong and how can I help?" "Tell me why you are feeling this way." Yes, you might feel as if you are talking to yourself, but it's a little different from that. When you take a compassionate approach to understanding yourself, you're actually operating as your higher self, the strong and truest version of your soul. The version of yourself that you most want to become on a full-time basis.

If you find it difficult to do this in your head, take the time to break it out into a journal entry. Very often writing about how we are feeling is far more powerful than just thinking about it.

As you are working through your emotions, know ahead of time that you are going to do five important things rather quickly: Understand. Identify. Resolve. Forgive and Move On.

ONE: UNDERSTAND

Understand what emotion your physical body is signaling. Is it anger? Sadness? Fear?

TWO: IDENTIFY

Identify which events or thoughts in your life triggered your body to provide you with those physical sensations. You may have to work backwards in time in your mind until it "clicks" both mentally and physically.

THREE: RESOLVE

Resolve the emotion. First determine if the event or thought that triggered the emotion is within your control, or not within your control. If it is outside of your control, say a prayer to God to take this feeling from you and provide healing where healing is needed. Then turn it over completely to God for Him to handle.

If it is within your control, determine what you can do to resolve the emotion and turn its energy into something that feels good within your soul. Each event and thought is different, but no matter what, act and respond lovingly to yourself and others. Tap into the Divine Virtues and Modalities of Mindful Thinking to guide your decision making. Does resolving the emotion related to an event require an apology or an explanation to someone? Does resolving the emotion require you to make peace with something you did in the past? If so, do it.

FOUR: FORGIVE

Forgive the event or thought. If the emotion happens to stem from an event that occurred in the past that cannot be repaired or redone, you can still make amends on a spiritual level by creating your own narrative to the story based on the transformative lesson you learned from it.

How do you wish the situation could have gone differently given what you realize now? Can you put a positive spin on the event? For example, if you stole something from someone, or lied, and later realized that you were not acting honestly, you could tell yourself something like: "even though I'm not proud of my actions, this situation has taught me the value of honesty. What happened in the past is not for nothing and I will use the experience to turn myself into a more honest person, one who will choose to not do something like this again in the future."

In doing this, you make it so that the event served an honorable purpose in your growth which will benefit your future interactions with others. As I mentioned earlier. It's not the events of our life that hurt us, it's the stories we attach to the events in our life that hurt us. If you were to instead beat yourself up about what you've done in the past, and call yourself "a terrible person who cannot be trusted," you might actually end up believing that about yourself, even if it's not true, and thoughts like that lead to self-sabotaging beliefs and actions. However, seeing that you put a positive spin on it, the next time you choose honesty over dishonesty, you'll get the personal proof that you need and will know for a fact that you are undoubtedly transforming into your higher self, and with that, your moral character is becoming stronger and stronger with each passing day-- which is something to be very proud of.

FIVE: MOVE ON

Move On. Now that you've resolved the source of your emotion, you have done your part, and it is okay to move on with your new understanding in its place. Dwelling on the past creates anxiety within us. We must remain forward focused on personal growth, and in order for personal growth to occur, we must create a loving environment within us where we are allowed to mess up and be imperfect. Praying to God for additional forgiveness and asking Him to remove any remaining negative emotions from within you is a great way to conclude your lesson.

Sometimes we experience several emotions at the same time. If you do your part to be mindful of your body's physical signs on a regular basis, then you shouldn't have too much trouble deciphering which emotions are tied to which events or thoughts going on in your life. However, if you continually ignore or push away the physical signs that your body is giving to you, you may find yourself very confused as to why you feel the way you do because you won't be able to determine which emotion was triggered by which event or thought. The same way a house needs to be kept clean daily in order to stay on top of managing the mess, so does your body, heart, and mind. Taking inventory of your emotions on a regular basis plays an important role in your ability to maintain your sobriety. Make your happiness and peace of mind a priority, and be sure to give yourself the attention you deserve.

The situations that you fear are rarely as bad as the fear itself. Don't be afraid to feel your feelings. If you already know ahead of time that you're going to treat yourself with respect, love, and forgiveness, then what is there to fear?

Sometimes in life, events arise out of nowhere that threaten to derail us, such as the loss of a loved one or a major life change. As upsetting as these events are, we know that they are bound to happen eventually, so the best way to prepare ourselves mentally and emotionally, is to set up a "Grief Plan" for ourselves to lean on when our emotions try to take over and send us spiraling out of control.

A Grief Plan is when you forecast as best you can, how you might feel when that event occurs, then pre-determine ahead of time what you want the outcome to be. For example, I dread the day when my Mother will die. She is my best friend and without her, my world would be missing something very special. However, I know that in life, people eventually need to head back home to Heaven and physically leave us for a while. (They never leave us spiritually though.)

I can forecast in my mind that I am going to need some time to lie in bed and just cry. I don't know for how long, but I'm going to say right now that I'd like to not lose myself in the sadness for longer than a few weeks to a month. Give or take. I'm pre-allowing myself to make room to feel my feelings, but I'm also stating ahead of time that I will not lose myself to them. In order to help me move out of my grief, I'm going to pre-plan honoring her memory and celebrating her life in many different creative ways throughout my life.

I'm creating positive things in my mind ahead of time that I know I can look forward to doing to pull myself out of my sadness. Having a Grief Plan in place will help me to get through the heavy emotions that this event will eventually bring. Doing this will comfort me at the beginning of my grieving knowing ahead of time, that as sad as it is, I'm going to be okay in the end.

If someone in your life dies suddenly and unexpectedly, or if you find yourself in the midst of a break up with someone you were in a relationship with, the first thing you should do before the initial shock wears off, is to quickly in your mind develop a Grief Plan so that the event does not trigger a relapse. State for the record, out loud even, that "This event will not cause me to relapse and I will not use it as an excuse to relapse." It is in high-stress times like these when you need to be vigilant and protective of your sobriety.

I'd like to take a little detour for a moment and talk about death. If you've lost a loved one in your life, perhaps due to an overdose, it's important for you to know, that often, souls choose their "checkout times." Meaning that before we're born, we choose when we want to return to Heaven.

Sometimes, the checkout time that is chosen is in direct relation to the role that person agreed to play in your life. Their death could be divinely timed to serve as a critical lesson for you, and its timing could have been planned in such a way so that you could use it as an opportunity for your recovery if you chose to do so.

Am I saying that all death is pre-planned and that free-will (a.k.a., the decisions we choose to make) play no role in when we depart this world? No. I do wish that I could say that with all certainty because it would make death hurt a little less, but I cannot. This is one of life's great mysteries that we'll only get the answer to once we get back to the other side and are filled with all the knowledge of the Universe once again.

For now though, just know that it does happen sometimes, and it's important to be open- minded to the possibility that someone's death could have been divinely pre-planned in order to help you grow and evolve. If you knew that a person's soul chose their death precisely to help you in some way, shape, or form, shouldn't you view that as a beautiful, selfless gift? Tara, for example, had a revelation at Ray's funeral that changed her life forever. In addition to that, in losing both her best friend and her boyfriend, a healthy, new environment was created for her where she was no longer surrounded by others who were using. Although these two events are extremely sad, they did happen, and they did play an important role in her recovery.

Did Eric, Ray, and Tara all choose to experience the journey of an addict together in this lifetime because their souls knew they needed to uncover and learn the lessons that only addiction can teach? Did Eric and Ray volunteer to live this life with her and checkout at a certain time because it was decided that would be a part of Tara's soul's growth plan? Only God, Ray, and Eric know for sure.

Don't shrug seemingly random events off as just something that happened. There's almost always a deeper meaning to things that we can't see or understand just yet, which time usually reveals. Instead of feeling as if things are always happening *to you*, try to find the gift and opportunity for growth in even the hardest of situations, and begin to understand that things could be happening *for you*. Yes, even in the hardest of situations like deaths, breakups, and sickness.

Now getting back to Grief Plans. You can create a Grief Plan for any event that you see coming down the pipeline. It doesn't need to be reserved only for death. For example, if you know that in a month, many people where you work are going to lose their jobs, instead of waiting to see if you'll be let go and how upset or anxious that will make you, create a plan ahead of time where you manage these types of feelings by looking forward to using that first week off as an opportunity to do things that will lift your spirits. These include things you couldn't do normally while working a full time schedule, like going for a walk mid-day, or meeting up with a friend for lunch.

You can also pre-plan to put a positive spin on the event by telling yourself that if you are let go, you will use this time to reevaluate what you are most passionate about in life and find an even better job than the one you just left behind. Doing this might even make you look forward to getting fired. As I keep saying, we create our own reality with our thoughts, so choosing good ones is so very important.

You can also create a similar type of plan for moments when your drug of choice might be staring you in the face. Before this situation even has the chance to occur, picture it happening in your mind. Then picture yourself being strong enough to say "no thanks, this isn't who I am anymore," refusing it, and walking away.

Creating a Grief Plan doesn't need to take more than a couple of minutes, but it could potentially save you from losing weeks, months, if not years of your life if you were to become consumed by your emotions and end up relapsing.

Now ask yourself, what events should you make a Grief Plan for? Grab a journal and make a list. This will help you to be prepared for future events if and when they happen. Keep in mind though that this exercise should not be done in such an extreme way that you start to imagine made-up scenarios that may never come true. It should be done in a way that will save you from stress and grief, and not create additional stress and worry in your life.

Most of this chapter has been about how to manage emotions, but what happens if you do end up in a situation where your drug of choice is right in front of you, tempting you to use again? First off, I hope you will remember what we talked about at the beginning of the book; that you are a soul on a journey of learning, and that the lessons and challenges that you don't master in this lifetime, will repeat in the next lifetime and the next, and the next, until you get it right.

As you are staring at your drug of choice, ask yourself if you want to master your lessons in this lifetime and be done with addiction forever, or do you want to live in this hell forever? If the answer is yes, that you want to get it right in this lifetime, immediately pray to God, right then and there, to give you the strength to reject the poison in front of you and physically walk away. This is when you need to trust that God is providing you with even more than what you just asked for. Feel his strength flowing through you, making you instantly stronger and able to resist anything. Picture yourself refusing it, and walking away, just like you pre-planned to do in your mind.

You can make these strategies work for you by owning the moment between thinking about using, and actually using. That little space, or pause, between thought and action is where your power lies and where God can work miracles. The longer you pause, the longer God has to work His magic. You are allowed to change the path you are on even when others are watching. You are allowed to take control and be the captain of your life. Each time you choose yourself and your future over using, you are reclaiming your personal power and strength.

It's important to recognize the crucial, pivotal, defining moments of your life for what they are, as they are happening. To do this, try viewing yourself outside of yourself as if you were watching a movie of your life. Watching the main character (you) make decisions that will carry them triumphantly to a better life which they deserve, or crash and burn yet again. Visualize in your mind the outcome you want for the main character, and be sure that your real-life actions always support that outcome.

If you're having a hard time figuring out if your actions will support or sabotage your sobriety goals, take a moment to forecast into the future what the consequences of the decision you're making will have in the long run. Decide what the worst case scenario is, and if you don't want that result, then don't go down that road. This process will get easier and easier to do the more you do it, until eventually you'll do it automatically.

Realize that each and every decision you make to stay sober throughout your life will lead you to the happy ending you most want for yourself. Having witnessed your struggles, the audience, which is yourself, God, your Angels, and your Spirit Guides, all cheer for you each time you succeed. You are creating a beautiful life for yourself with every single decision you make, both big and small.

CHAPTER 10

LESSON 7:
PASSION & PURPOSE

I've been talking a lot about learning lessons through-out this book, and how that's the main purpose of our lives, but there's actually another major purpose to life that's just as important, and that is fulfilling the promise we made to God before we were born to love, help, and teach others.

You see, there's a master plan that God has for all of humanity, complete with timelines, roles, influence, and outcomes. The world may seem chaotic, and random, but it's really not. Everything has a right timing, place, and order that was designed to support your learning and growth throughout your life, and to help others with their learning and growth too.

Each one of us plays an important role in God's plan. The contributions we make to the lives of others while we're alive, helps to keep people on their predesigned path, which helps God to achieve His bigger picture for us all.

Each one of us possesses unique gifts from God, or talents or traits that come naturally to us. These gifts can range from being artistic, to being mathematically minded. Or perhaps you're musically inclined, or spiritual, or especially caring, organized, or social, or you write, cook, grow, or build things really well.

It may seem to you that there isn't anything particularly special about you, but you'd be wrong. There's a trap that many people fall into, and that's believing the lie, that just because something comes easily to them, they don't have anything special to offer the world. The reason why so many people believe this is because they've possessed their gifts for so long that they've ended up taking them for granted and assume that other people are probably just as good at those same things too. Don't become blind to your gifts.

This happened to me, and if it weren't for a very talented psychic named Angel Amy located in Danvers, MA, I don't think I would have recognized my talents for what they actually were; special gifts from God. My reading with her, which I recorded on my phone, went something like this:

"Right away I can tell that you are a very grounded person, and I have the overwhelming sensation that you are a natural born healer." (To which I very much agreed).

"You are not exactly on your life path." (At the time I was working hard to start up a charitable coffee company called We the People Coffee & Tea, which empowered our customers to give back to local nonprofits within their favorite city.)

"Your life path is strongly related to healing and progressing people who feel stuck."

"I see a book. You're going to get published in your lifetime. I feel that you have a natural ability to write. Are you a writer?"

To which I responded: "I can, but it's not my first thing." (Kind of funny considering that right now you're reading a book that I wrote myself.)

Looking back into my childhood, I have a memory of sitting on my bed, writing a short story, and being amazed at how when you change one little word in a sentence, it alters the entire meaning and tone of the whole message. This memory proves to me that I've always been really interested in writing, I just never viewed myself as "good" at writing simply because it came naturally to me. So I want you to think about the talents you possess that you may be overlooking and taking for granted, because that is what makes you special and you don't even realize it.

Similar, but separate from our talents, is something called passion, which is directly related to your purpose in life. Your purpose being the way in which you contracted with God to help others. Your purpose in life can also be related to the lessons your soul needs to learn during your lifetime. You see, we have two different kinds of purposes in our life. One serves us personally as lessons and the other serves other people by helping them. Our two main purposes can occur separately, or together at the same time. Often, in helping others, we help ourselves and the lessons are found in the giving itself. It's a really beautiful and joyful experience when the two combine.

Our passions are the things that we are most interested in. Some people find that they have many passions, and others feel like they have none. And sometimes people know very specifically what they're most passionate about.

My motivation for starting We the People Coffee & Tea was because I had a passion for wanting to inspire people to create the change they wish to see in the world. Which is essentially what I'm still doing now, but in a different and more profound way because I get to help people create the change they wish to see within themselves, and that positive energy ends up trickling out into the world and ends up making it a better place in so many different ways.

I believe that if I can get you to discover and embrace your talents and passions, then you'll begin to see that God put you on this planet for a very specific reason; to change the world by helping others in your own unique way.

There's a major lesson I've learned throughout my life when it comes to trying to find your purpose, and that is, there's a big difference between what you *think* you're supposed to do, and what you are *meant* to do. I "wasted" a lot of time trying to do things in a way that society "expected," but once I stopped being afraid to be different, that's when I felt most proud of myself. I stopped being afraid to let my spiritual side show, and I stopped keeping my Intuitive Claircognizance under wraps and began to see it for what it was; one of my unique God-given gifts. I stopped being afraid to step up and get involved in people's lives. I stopped being afraid to show people radical amounts of love.

Success to me is being happy and at peace within yourself, while getting to help others at the same time. That is something that money could never buy. Of course, the money that may come along with following your passion is nice, but that's just a bonus in my eyes.

There's another important lesson that I learned on my quest to discovering my purpose, which is that you don't need to look further than yourself for success, because what you are naturally good at, and what you are naturally passionate about, is *exactly* what makes you special, and what makes you special, makes you different, and what makes you different is *exactly* what the world needs. So stop ignoring that part of you! You probably don't even realize that you're doing it. I didn't. It's waiting there, just beneath the surface. Waiting for you to see it for what it really is. Your special gift from God. You just need to put all expectations of yourself aside, and take an honest look within.

Find comfort in your heart knowing that it's okay to be different and it's okay to "fail" as you dare to try new things, because there really isn't such a thing as failure, only learning. I've "failed" thousands of times, and each failure has taught me something important which brought me closer to my true calling. The only way to truly fail is to give up.

As long as you're afraid of being judged by others, you are destined to live a life built for you by society and not by God and your heart, leading you to feel like you're trying to force a square peg into a round hole. Being truthful about who you are is vital to living a life of authenticity.

Your purpose in life doesn't necessarily need to be related to your full-time career, but it's always nice when it can be. It could be something you do as a hobby, or on a volunteer basis, or on a part-time basis on nights and weekends. Again, don't worry about what people might expect or think of you, big or small, just do what makes you happiest, whenever you can do it and do it with love for helping others in your heart.

This reminds me of a near death experience story I once read about a middle-aged man who crossed over and met God. During his life review, he got to see that his job as a crossing guard was being highlighted as one of the defining moments of his life. God knew how seriously he took his job, and how he did it with genuine passion in his heart for protecting little children. In the human world a job like this might not be very glamorous or command much respect, but in God's eyes, this man was a superstar because he did his job with such love in his heart for others. Whatever you do, do it because you want to serve people somehow, then own it! Really own it!

Another way that God hopes we will help with His plan, is to spread love and kindness to others wherever we go. We can help others by doing the simplest of things in our day-to-day lives, like holding the door open for someone, or picking up something they accidentally dropped, letting someone merge in front of you in traffic, or smiling, or taking a moment to talk to them, or give a genuine compliment. There are unlimited opportunities to help and love one another each and every day. You just need to look around to try and find and create them, and resist the tendency to get caught up in the hustle and bustle of the human world.

Don't allow social labels to define you, or become a crutch for you to use as an excuse to hold you back, use it as a reason to thrive! Along my journey I've also learned that God places us exactly where we need to be based on the ways in which our lives need to be influenced and where our help is needed. Perhaps you feel that you aren't where you want to be in your life right now, but on the contrary, you are *precisely* where you need to be. This is your unique path and it was designed just for you.

Bloom where you are planted and love your life exactly as it is right now. Don't fall into the trap of comparing your life to the lives of others. We are all on our own journeys, and even though our lives may look different to the naked eye, we're all traveling toward the same destination, toward a collective consciousness of unconditional love for ourselves and others. Each one of us in this world is part of the greater whole of God. It's just that some people haven't realized it yet. By simply reading this book, and deciding to expand your consciousness, you are one of the lucky ones who is gearing up to experience life as it was meant to be lived.

Be the type of person who no matter where you go, adds value to the spaces and lives around you. Serving others with love in your heart is the best way to see that you really matter in this world. In serving others we find ourselves. We are all teachers and students at the same time.

Who or what do you see in your community that could use your help? Keep in mind, that just because someone doesn't flat out ask you for help, doesn't mean they don't need it. How can you use your talents and experience to support a cause you care deeply about? I challenge you to take some time to really think about this, and then take action and get involved in a way that excites you the most. The world urgently needs your contribution!

No matter which choice you make, or direction you decide to go in, you will always make the right decision because when you let God guide your heart, your purpose and destiny will always be fulfilled. Even if something doesn't work out as planned, God is simply preparing you for even greater things to come. Remember not to get caught up in the results; live in the present moment and enjoy the journey right here and now.

CHAPTER 11

LESSON 8:
THE IMPORTANCE
OF DAILY RITUALS

If you're sick and tired of all the BS this human world brings, then there's one way to avoid it, and that's to stop living as a human, and to start living as a soul, which is your truest form anyhow, which is why this works. When you begin to live life as your higher self, you are essentially returning yourself, to yourself.

Stop getting all tangled up in the weeds of human thinking and behavior and rise up and above the noise and chaos. You don't need to suffer. The struggle actually isn't "real" at all. It's just perceived that way by our egos and human minds.

Do all you can to integrate what you've just read into your life. Even when you're done reading this book I hope you will make continuous growth a part of your life too. It's not hard, but it does take discipline and a commitment to nurturing the growth of your higher self on a regular basis. Of course I am here to help you do this if you want to work directly with me, but in addition to that there's an important habit that you need to put in place in order to stay centered, calm, focused, and growing while living as a human, and that is to develop daily rituals that will keep you grounded, centered, and aligned with your higher self. The same way you shower every day to wash the dirt off your body, you need to engage in one or more of these rituals each day to keep the dirt off your soul.

ONE: PRAY.

In order to experience real, lasting change, you need to connect with God, or your Angels, or your Spirit Guides on a daily basis. This one is non-negotiable and needs to happen daily. Think of yourself like a phone whose battery gets worn out by the end of each day. You can't keep letting the world deplete you of your energy without plugging back into the main power source to recharge.

God, The Creator, is the main power source of the entire Universe, and without that connection, humans feel lost and confused, like a tiny boat trying to navigate the stormy seas alone, which over time gets really exhausting.

Praying is often associated with organized religion, which is why I feel that many people have gotten away from it. Prayer though, is simply the transmission of our energy to God, and from God back to us. Prayer, like a divine phone call, allows us to directly communicate with God.

Prayer doesn't need to be fancy. It doesn't need to take long, you just need to speak to God or your Angels or your

Spirit Guides the same way you would a trusted best friend. Your conversations can range from casual and quick, like: "Please help me to have a good day today and see the good in others" to serious and longer like: "God I feel weak and I really need you to fill me with your strength. I feel lost and trapped in my own head, please help me to find peace. Please help me to find joy in my life and a reason to live. Help me to understand and accept your plan."

Your prayer can be as short or as long as you want, and you can speak in your head or out loud. It doesn't matter because God understands your intention and is not listening with his ears, He is listening with His heart, the same way you are communicating with Him from your heart.

You don't need to kneel down to pray as many of us are taught, but if it makes you feel closer to God, then by all means do it. For the record, you could pray to God while on the toilet and your prayer would still be heard loud and clear and God would not take offense to the location. He's just happy to hear from you no matter where you "place the call."

Personally though, sometimes while praying I like to get really into it, and give it a more ceremonious feel. This especially helps me when I am feeling that what I have to say is of great importance to me. Before kneeling to begin my prayer I might light a white candle, or burn some incense or essential oil. I might burn some Palo Santo sticks or sage to remove any lingering negative energy from myself or the room.

Note: burning sage smells similar to marijuana and may be a trigger for some people. However, Palo Santo sticks (also known as holy wood) have a sweet, woodsy smell and do the same thing to remove negative energy.

Personally, for my longer, more ceremonious prayers, I like to bless myself with the cross before diving into it, but you in no way need to do that if you don't want to. I start my prayer by saying "Dear God" or "Dear Heavenly Father" and then I spill my guts out to Him. For my shorter, more immediate conversations with God, I don't bother to make the sign of the cross because, more often than not, I'm talking to Him throughout the day as I'm doing something else like driving, or working... and yes, sometimes even while on the toilet or in the shower. God is wherever you are, so you can literally pray wherever you might be.

While praying, tell God how you're feeling, what you're confused about, what you want answers about, what you feel you need most in your life. There's one thing that people do wrong while talking to God though, and that is to pray in a way that is devoid of love and makes them the victim or pushes blame onto other people.

For example if someone prayed: "Dear God, Sally is really frustrating me, could you please have her position at work get moved to a different location so I don't have to deal with her anymore?" This prayer will never get answered because the person praying is not taking responsibility for their personal growth, and that's the name of the game while we're here on Earth.

The prayer will get answered if it is presented in this way though: "Dear God, Sally is really frustrating me, and whenever I'm around her I find myself becoming very angry. Could you please help me to strengthen my patience and find a way to communicate with her to let her know how I'm feeling without hurting her feelings?" Do you see the difference?

Before we go much further, I want to tell you a little more about your Angels and Spirit Guides. In addition to God, we have so many other divine beings that are by our side each and every day. This is an incredibly in-depth topic, and an entire book could be written on it, so I'll just keep this simple for now.

We all have various Angels who guide us. There are three main types of Angels which are your "traditional" Angels, Guardian Angels, and Archangels. Guardian Angels protect us personally, and Archangels protect all of humanity. Guardian Angels have never been human before, so they provide us with a guiding viewpoint of utmost divinity.

We all have Spirit Guides that watch over us every day of our lives as well. Spirit Guides have been human before and therefore understand what it's like to live this challenging human experience.

We each have several Angels and Guides that are assigned to us before we are born. As I mentioned earlier in the book, because we have freewill to reject help from anyone, typically, these divine beings are not allowed to step in to help us unless we specifically invite them into our lives by praying to them asking them for assistance. So be sure to take the time to pray to them as well.

After praying to God, your Angels, and Guides, look for signs and synchronicities that your prayers are being acknowledged or answered. If you don't get exactly what you prayed for, it usually means that whatever you're going through is an important part of your learning journey and therefore you should embrace it, accept it, and learn from it. Only then will your prayers be answered by what you have discovered from it.

God is so good, confusing, and mysterious at times, but so good! I have "a-ha" moments when I look back at situations and see how their past outcomes helped to create the perfect scenarios and opportunities in my present life. That's when I say to God, "oh, okay, I see what you did there." It feels really good to know that He has a perfect plan for us all and that we really don't need to try and control anything and can just relax knowing that everything is unfolding just as it should. This allows you to finally unload the weight of the world from your shoulders.

When is the best time to pray? Anytime really, but it's really powerful to do it when your eyes first open in the morning and are about to close again at night. Doing this instead of reaching for your phone and getting caught up in the nonsense of the human world allows you to claim and protect your personal power. Praying allows you to set your intentions by asking for what you need, proclaiming what you are thankful for, and praying for others who are in need of help and support.

When I wake in the morning, the first thing I do is give thanks for some of the things in my life that I am grateful for. This sets the tone for the day focused on abundance and not of lack. If I happen to have an important event to go to, or I'm facing a particular challenge, I ask for what I need around that. When it's just another normal day for me, I ask God to help make me a mirror of his unconditional love and do his work throughout my day. When I'm done praying I feel that I have a boost of energy and my mind is clearer. I'm also more optimistic and view the day as a gift full of opportunity.

I also like to pray to God as I'm falling asleep. I like to recap the parts of the day that stuck with me and ask for help or clarity where needed. I also like to pray for the people I've encountered throughout the day who are struggling in some way or another. Then I pray for a restful sleep, I thank God and tell Him that I love Him. When we sleep our minds are more open to receiving messages and information from God, our Angels, and Spirit Guides, so often, when I wake up, I seem to have the answers or power that I was seeking in my prayers from the night before.

Make prayer a part of your daily routine and your life will improve drastically!

TWO: CREATE A SACRED SPACE FOR YOURSELF

The environment in which you live has the ability to bring peace into your life, or anxiety. When you're in your space, whether it be an entire home, or just a room, or even just a bed, be sure that you make your space work for you by keeping it clean, organized, and visually appealing to your senses.

My friend Tara was telling me the other day about a saying she has for why she makes her bed every morning, which is: "messy bed, messy head." After you wake up and connect with God, and step out of bed for the day, it's a good idea to make your bed. Making your bed sets the tone for the rest of the day, and even if you don't do anything else all day, at least you've done this, and get to crawl back into a freshly made bed at the end of the day. Which is so much better than trying to get comfortable in a jumbled mess of sheets. Investing in a nice looking and feeling bedspread, sheets, and fun throw pillows will make it all the more exciting to make too.

Keep your space organized and clean. Try to create a space for everything, because when everything has its place, it won't end up on the floor in a pile of visual chaos.

Right-brained, more creative people, tend to find it harder than left-brained analytical types to stay organized. I can guarantee though, that your mind will feel more at ease living in an open, airy, organized space over a confined, cluttered mess of a space no matter who you are. If you're the creative type, just do your best to tidy up as often as possible, and if you're the analytical type, do your best to not let anxiety overtake you when things get messy or don't get done right away. Remember it's all about balance, not perfection.

THREE: YOGA

Yoga is another thing that you should think about working into your daily routine. As humans we are physical beings and therefore we need to move our bodies.

When we exercise and move our bodies, neurotransmitters like dopamine and serotonin trigger feel-good emotions in our brains. Because of this, exercise works as a natural antidepressant.

Yoga is a great way to do this because it's a very spiritual, calming way to provide movement to your body. It also strengthens and stretches your muscles at the same time. We have to remember that our bodies are just on loan to us for this one lifetime, so if you want it to last, you need to take care of it by moving it regularly and watching what kind of food and nutrients you put into it.

FOUR: MEDITATION

Meditation is different from praying. Praying is mostly a "two way" conversation between you, God, your Angels, and Guides. Meditation is when you allow yourself time in the day to sit somewhere quietly, for five minutes or more, with no distractions, closing your eyes and clearing your mind of any thoughts. This gives your conscious mind a chance to relax and be still which helps reduce anxiety.

Some people like to ring a Tibetan singing bowl at the beginning of their meditation, some people like to play soft meditation music, and some prefer silence. When meditating, if you find that your mind runs all over the place from one thought to another, that's okay, and it's completely normal, just take a moment to bring yourself back to center and focus on your breathing. While meditating I like to picture a triangle between my eyes (with the point facing upwards towards God, my higher self, and my "third eye," keeping me connected to love, intuition, and wisdom). I try to keep my focus centered on the empty, peaceful silence found within this triangle. Allow yourself to sit silently, and become enveloped by the healing power of God's unconditional loving energy. Feel God entering your soul and allow Him to repair any part of you that feels broken.

FIVE: JOURNALING

Another great practice to take up is journaling. Journaling is the activity of writing down your thoughts and feelings into a book that is dedicated specifically to you. Doing this allows us to reach into our minds and hearts and pull out all of the things that are cluttering up our head and heart space. So often when we don't purge our thoughts and feelings onto paper, it feels as if they are locked up inside of us, swirling around in our heads, with no way to escape. Once you release them by bringing them out into the world and onto paper, you can finally feel free of them, and often, when you write them down, you begin to see your problems in a completely new light and solutions begin to come to you which may have never occurred to you before.

When writing, you can pretend that you are writing to a best friend whom you can trust with your deepest, darkest secrets. Or you can write to your higher self, or use it as another way to pray to God. Whatever feels best to you is how you should approach it.

I also suggest using a journal to answer any questions from previous chapters in this book, like the ones in Chapter 8 for example. Also, if while reading this book you'd like to expand your thoughts on a particular topic, doing so by writing in a journal is a great way to keep track of your thoughts and questions.

There are so many beautiful notebooks available that can be used as a journal. If you are worried about privacy, journals with key locks or combination locks are available.

SIX: SNAPSHOTS OF HAPPINESS

There is something that I began doing in my life a few years ago that has really improved it, and that is to regularly take snapshots of happy, joyful, special, or unique moments that I come across in my life.

Now when I do this, I'm not using an actual camera, or phone, but I'm using my senses and memory. For example, if I'm walking down the street and I notice two people engaging in a deep, meaningful belly laugh with each other, I'll recognize that moment for how special it is in terms of human connection, and I'll take a mental picture of it and consciously store the joyful feeling of it in my heart's memory.

Some other examples might be the sound of kids laughing and playing, birds chirping, the look of love in a person's eyes, someone dancing around all goofy or someone helping another person. Taking mental snapshots of the world around me keeps me living in the present moment, which is the only moment we truly have in life, isn't it? When you do this, over time, you may not remember everything you took a "picture" of, but the positive energy will remain in your heart, helping you to feel happier and more optimistic because you'll begin to realize just how much beauty is around you each and every day. Many people spend their days scanning the world for what's wrong and bad with it. If this is you, change your world today by starting to look for what's right and good in the world. This might be hard at first, but the more you do it, the easier and more automatic it will become.

SEVEN: SOUL VISION

Our senses help us to navigate the world and keep us safe, but as we talked about in the chapter titled: the Modalities of Mindful Thinking, very often, the way we process information gets in the way of us seeing the truth and beauty in life. I want to challenge you to override this default way of thinking though by making "Soul Vision" part of your daily routine.

Soul Vision is when you consciously decide to stop judging people based on their visual appearance or material possessions and instead, pause a little longer to recognize and feel the energy of their soul. This will help you to see the human race as being connected within a collective of divine energy instead of as individuals competing against one another based on our differences and achievements.

For example, one day I was at the airport and I was sitting watching the people around me begin to board the plane. First came the busy business man. I could tell that he was feeling anxious for his trip as he fumbled for his phone. Then there was the exhausted mother trying her best to keep it together as she herded her children to the boarding area. Then there was the sad looking elderly man, and the self-conscious pre-teen looking in her compact mirror applying makeup. All of this energy makes up the human experience, and we've all had similar emotions at one time or another. I knew that even though all of these people looked different than me, they too, were all simply trying to make it through this thing called life as best they could, and that is something we all have in common.

CHAPTER 12:

ROADBLOCKS

The evolution of a soul can be explained as a series of steps, where a person moves from a "third dimension" (3D) way of thinking, where in the physical world the ego is fully in control, to a "fourth dimension" (4D) way of thinking, where most of the transformation to higher self takes place, to a "fifth dimension" (5D) way of thinking, where a person lives with a mindful heart, completely in control of their thoughts and emotions, replacing the fearful human ego with God's energy of unconditional love.

In the 5D world, a person lives as their higher self, no longer connected to the low vibrational energy of the 3D physical world, as they have now transitioned to living within the high vibrational energy of the spiritual world. In the 5D world a person can live in peace, mostly unphased by the chaos of the "human world."

Moving from 3D to 5D takes discipline and continual commitment to changing the self, so you have to be willing to completely give up who you are now, in order to become the person you were meant to be. Even then, the ego never fully goes away, it just gets smaller and quieter.

Did you know that very often, people who become addicted to drugs or alcohol are closer to living in the 5D world than they think? Often turning to substances to heal some form of pain they feel inside, they are very much aware that something is "wrong" with the 3D world, and a soul cannot understand that something is "wrong," unless it first understands what is "right."

If this is the case for you, it means that your soul already has inherent knowledge of the 5D world, and therefore, when you were born and shoved into the 3D human world, with all its twisted, upside-down belief systems, you had a harder time than most people adjusting to it, because deep down, your soul already knew the truth of how it should be.

This means that if you keep putting effort into evolving and growing, you'll reach the 5D world faster than most other souls on the planet. Not that it's a competition, but your soul *could be* more "advanced" than most other people living in the 3D world. You'll never know it though unless you start to live in a way that moves you away from the things that keep tripping you up by aligning your mind and your heart with God and the loving laws of the Universe. Engaging in self-reflection, unlearning limiting behaviors, thoughts, and beliefs and committing yourself to continual learning is the only way to do this.

If you're ready to embark on your own personal spiritual journey, let's take a deeper look at some roadblocks you may stumble across so that you can be prepared for them.

EGO

The biggest obstacle we face in life, is ourselves. At the end of the day, that's really the only person we're battling against. Or better said, we're battling against our own fearful egos; egos that take personal offense to everything others say and do. Egos that talk us out of attempting to achieve anything because it believes that if we stay small, we won't fail, and therefore won't get hurt. Egos that judge others to try and make us feel better about ourselves. Egos that put up walls to keep others out, and us in. Egos that make us feel unworthy of love.

Your ego will look for so many ways to sabotage your growth process because when you're brave enough to look inward, critique yourself, and uncover the ways in which you are imperfect, the ego's red flag goes up because it hates being anything less than perfect. You must be strong enough and smart enough to notice when your ego is trying to take over and keep you stuck in your current comfort zone by offering up excuses, tempting you to procrastinate and not take action, and supporting old distorted thinking habits and beliefs that will derail your progress.

STRESS

Another roadblock that will come up is life itself. Life has a way of dropping stress bombs on us when we least expect it, which can threaten our peace of mind. To combat this we need to make sure we have strong spiritual and mental tools in place to control our thoughts and not let our thoughts control us.

You can't heal yourself if you're always running away from yourself, so if you want to get to know and become the truest version of yourself, you'll need to stop trying to numb the pain of the 3D world with alcohol or drugs in an attempt to try and escape from it. Abusing substances keeps you trapped in the 3D world which ends up being less of an escape and more like a self-inflicted prison. Good news though, as you evolve, the less you'll feel the need to numb because the pain of the human world will have very little control over you.

FEAR OF PAIN

Healing the past takes time and energy. It involves digging deeply, openly, and honestly within yourself to better understand your personal life experiences, the stories and the emotions you have tied to those experiences.

Some people fear that doing this might reopen old wounds and cause them emotional pain. The thing is, the only way to heal a wound is to open it up again, and clean it out properly, because right now it's not really healed. It's festering with decay just beneath the surface. You've held onto your wounds for so long that you've gotten accustomed to the pain. You can either live in denial about that, and live with the nagging discomfort of it the rest of your life, or you can be honest with yourself, do what's best for you in the long run, and take care of your wounds now so that they heal up in a nice, healthy way that will leave you feeling free and liberated. I'm here to make the healing process as pain-free as possible for you.

It takes practice to implement the Divine Virtues into your life in such a way that you can understand when ego is interfering and manipulating you again. To do that you need to understand who you are as a person and what you stand for. You'll never use just one virtue at a time, but all of them at once, and therefore you need to fully understand what each one means and why they're important to you. After all, these will become the foundation of your moral character.

FEAR OF THE UNKOWN

Humans are creatures of habit, which makes many people fear change. With addiction though, I can guarantee you that you've already lived through the hardest part and that it will only get easier from here. The hardest part isn't the spiritual journey you're on, the hardest part was when you were completely lost to the darkness, before you felt the glimmer of hope in your heart that you have now. Even if you feel that the glimmer is small and flickering, you still have it. Action and commitment to your personal growth is what will ignite that flame within you to burn even brighter. God's love is like a beacon of light that always guides everyone safely back to shore.

You have to believe with all your heart that the best part of your life has yet to come and that the future is always going to be better than the past.

Thinking about all the elements that need to come together to facilitate a spiritual transformation like this can be overwhelming, which by the way, your ego will try to use as an excuse to keep you stagnant, still, and locked into your old life, but you don't need to worry about that at all. Yes it's challenging, but with the right teacher to help guide you through the process, it can actually be fun, interesting, enjoyable, and incredibly uplifting.

As a Spiritual Wellness Mentor, it's my life's mission to help move people out of the 3D world, and into the 5D world so that they can stop hurting and finally start living! I invite you to contact me via the contact page on my website to learn more about my Spiritual Wellness Coaching program called the Mindful Heart Project®. If you want to make a powerful, lasting change in your life, I would consider it an honor to play a role in your transformation.

CHAPTER 13

CONCLUSION

As a Claircognizant, Intuitive Healer, I am naturally also an Empath who can feel the pain of others as if it were my own. This is a gift I've had for my entire life, and while it can be emotionally draining at times, it helps me to understand just how much the human race is struggling and suffering and how transformative and freeing the right knowledge can be to a person.

In reading this book, I pray that you are filled with so much more hope than you had when you first began reading it, because having hope for a better future is where your journey begins. My deepest wish for you is that this is just the beginning of your spiritual journey and that you keep learning and growing without fear of failure, and think more about all the things that could go right in your life, and less about what could go wrong. When we focus on what we *do* want in life, that's what we end up getting, so be mindful to not focus on what you *don't* want or you'll end up getting more of that.

Energy flows, where focus goes. For example, instead of saying to yourself fearfully "I don't want to relapse again," focus on saying to yourself "I want to live a beautiful life where I don't need to use substances to feel happy." If you focus on and visualize relapse, that's what you'll get. If you focus on and visualize a beautiful life, that's what you'll get. If you come away from this book having learned only one thing, I hope it will be the understanding of how powerful your thoughts really are. Always be mindful of your thoughts, because they are very transformative and they truly create your reality.

In this book you learned a bit about me, who I am, what I believe in, and how I would love to continue to be a part of your personal and spiritual transformation journey. Now let's revisit some of the other things we learned throughout this book.

In Chapter 4 you learned that organized religion doesn't tell us the whole truth and that so much more can be learned from people who have had near death experiences. Stories of unconditional love, destiny, spirit families, and God's master plan for each and every one of us. Most importantly, you learned that your greatest challenges in life were pre-planned and pre-chosen by you based on the lessons your soul knew it needed to learn in this lifetime, which is incredibly empowering!

In Chapter 5 you learned the concept of what it means to live on a higher level, the importance of being your own best friend and the value of putting out positive, loving energy into the world to help attract opportunities to you.

You learned about living fearlessly, mirroring God's love, and trusting His plan for you. You learned that you were born perfect, but how fear of the human world was instilled in you from a young age by the people and influences around you. You learned about ancestral trauma and how breaking the cycle of fear can heal thousands of people, including yourself.

In Chapters 6 and 7 you learned about the Divine Virtues and the Modalities of Mindful Thinking, and how they end up becoming the foundation of your moral compass, guiding your decision making; spiritual virtues like forgiveness, courage, humility, honesty, faith, patience, simplicity, and gratitude, and thinking modalities like interpretation, perception, intention, and response.

In Chapter 8 you learned about the importance of self-reflection and self-examination as it pertains to your personal growth. You put some thought into the questions asked, and learned about how much power is actually gained, not lost, by surrendering your life completely over to God.

In Chapter 9 you learned strategies for avoiding relapse; how to use your body as an early warning system to alert you that something is brewing beneath the surface that needs your attention. The process for decoding what it means, the process for resolving it, and a process for letting it go. You learned the value of having a "grief plan" and the "power of the pause" and how pretending to be the star of your own life can help you to stay sober.

In Chapter 10 you learned about the trap that people often fall into when trying to discover their talents and passions, and I shared with you the lessons I learned while searching for my purpose. You learned the best way to find yourself, why the world needs your unique contribution, and how there's no way to get this wrong.

In Chapter 11 you learned the importance of keeping daily rituals and how they can help you to overcome the madness of the human world, quiet your own thoughts, and steer you clear of relapsing. You learned specific techniques, concepts, and activities that you can incorporate into your own life to keep your mind, heart, and spirit aligned with God and your higher self.

In Chapter 12 you also learned about some of the roadblocks you may experience as you make your way through your spiritual journey and how to overcome them victoriously.

My wish for you, now that you're almost done reading this book, is that you'll be able to view the world with a fresh set of eyes, and a renewed heart for all that you encounter. I hope that you've discovered a new gentleness toward yourself full of forgiveness, patience, and love. I hope that you see the opportunity, and potential in each and every new day, and in each and every person you meet along the way. I hope you no longer allow the human world to determine how your life is going to be. I hope you no longer seek your joy and happiness from external sources and realize that it comes from within, from God's unconditional love that radiates from the inside out. I hope you view life as the miracle and gift that it really is and I hope you feel as strong as you actually are.

Writing this book for you has been an incredible honor. I hope that you will connect with me on Facebook, Instagram, and Twitter and share your stories of newfound hope and success with me. I may even use your story to inspire others.

If you don't want our journey together to end here, please reach out to me so that we can keep learning and growing together. I offer a Spiritual Wellness Coaching program called the Mindful Heart Project ® that I'd love to tell you more about.

Warmest blessings for a beautiful life,

-Nicole

YOU CAN FIND ME HERE:

FACEBOOK:
https://www.facebook.com/NicoleMolloy11/

INSTAGRAM:
https://www.instagram.com/nicole_molloy/

TWITTER:
https://twitter.com/NicoleMolloy11

WEBSITE:
www.nicolemolloy.com/contact

SHARE THE LOVE! If you'd like to give a free digital copy of this book to a friend, send them this link: https://www.nicolemolloy.com/freedigitalcopy/

THE MIRACLE OF HOW
THIS BOOK CAME TO BE

'd like to share a personal story with you about a time when I completely turned my entire life over to God, trusting that He would provide what I needed as long as it was in alignment with my life's path... and how if I hadn't done that, this book may not have been written.

As I mentioned earlier in the book, a few years ago, I was running a charitable coffee company called We the People Coffee & Tea which allowed our customers to donate a percentage of their purchase to local nonprofits within their community. I spent four years working to grow the company, but in the end, lack of funding caused me to have to shut it down. However, even before the company was to close, something inside of me realized that I wanted to do more than simply facilitate donations to charities; I wanted to work directly with people in the world who needed help getting "unstuck" in their lives. At the time I largely ignored this personal revelation because I was too invested in We the People Coffee to change my focus.

One day, a couple of months after my revelation, I was feeling stressed. We the People Coffee's financial situation wasn't looking so great, and I was starting to think that

I would have to shut the company down. To manage my stress, I carved out some "self-care" time in my schedule and booked an appointment for a massage. If there's one thing I'm good at, it's the ability to just let all my stresses go and enjoy a good massage. However, this massage was different. As I laid on my stomach getting my back massaged, I received an intuitive message that kept repeating throughout the entire hour long massage. "You need to help guide people. Moral compass. Lost. Teach." Not only were these words repeating over and over again in my head, throughout the massage, but my soul felt as if it were on fire! Not as if my skin were on fire, but a warmth that radiated from my heart, to my head, and from my heart to my arms and down to my toes. This was a full body message that I could not ignore. It felt as if my mind and body were in overdrive. (So much for relaxing.)

When the massage was over, I decided to go for a walk outside to try and process all that just happened. As I walked down the sidewalk, I asked myself "is what just happened real, or did I make all of it up? What was that?" Almost immediately after having that thought, a flag, which was hanging outside of a retail shop, blew in the wind and slapped me in the face. I put my hands up to push it away, and as I turned to look at the shop, my jaw dropped. There hanging on the display outside of the shop were several decorative compass roses. I couldn't believe it. I had just received an hour long intuitive message about how it's my mission to help people awaken their inner guidance and moral compass, and there I was having just been literally slapped in the face, made to look at the display of compasses, as if God were saying to me, "Yes, what just happened is very real." I went into the store and ended up buying one of the decorative compasses to hang in my living room to keep me inspired. I knew my mission now.

I went home, designed a compass inspired logo and trademarked a name that resonated with what I felt I was being called to do. I had no idea what I was going to do with it all, but at this point I was just following God's lead. This is how the Mindful Heart Project was born.

I still couldn't focus on the Mindful Heart Project though because We the People Coffee was still in business. Over the course of the next few months, I tried a few more things to save the coffee company from going under, but it didn't work out, and eventually I made the announcement to my customers that the company was shutting down. At the time my Daughter was just an infant, so after that happened I decided to take a break from the chaos of running a business to spend some quality time with her. Eventually though I felt the need to create something again… I knew *what* God wanted me to do, I just didn't know *how* exactly. Not to mention I was feeling a bit nervous about starting another business. I needed guidance. I felt lost and confused, but kept the faith that God would provide the direction I needed.

Then one evening, as I was scrolling through Instagram, I stumbled upon an advertisement for a writing program that promised to help heart centered healers write a book in just three months, and then use that book to help launch a coaching practice that would allow them to make a living helping others. I clicked on the link to learn more about the program. Still interested, I submitted my application. In order to get accepted into the program, you needed to pass a series of four interviews. With each interview I passed I was getting more and more excited to finally understand how the Mindful Heart Project could begin to take shape. At the end of the third interview is when you learn how much the program costs, so that on the fourth interview, if you're still interested, you can pay for it over the phone right then and there. This is a sales tactic, but it works to keep people from getting off the phone and never coming back again to fulfill their dreams. So even though I thought it was a little pushy, I understood that it was for my own benefit. The cost of the book writing program? $14,000. Yep. That's not a typo. It cost $14,000 and I had 5 days to come up with the money.

I got off the phone in total sticker shock! Where in the world was I going to find $14,000? I had no one that I could ask for the money because I had already borrowed quite a bit of money from family and friends to fund my coffee company. Anyone that might have given me money was no longer an option. I decided to ask acquaintances if they knew anyone that might be interested in funding my book. Day after day. No after no, I was getting more and more disappointed… and more and more desperate to find this money. I knew from that day at the massage that I was being called by God to do this work. How was I going to make it happen? Frustrated, I began to cry. Alone in my bedroom I began to pray to God, "Dear God, if it is your will for me to write this book, you need to have the money for this program find its way to me easily and quickly (at this point I needed to come up with the money in just two days). If I'm supposed to help people for a living, you need to send this money to me because I don't want to feel this stressed out anymore. I'm leaving it in your hands now."

After saying that prayer and releasing all of my concerns, expectations, and worry over to God, I completely detached myself from the outcome because I trusted in my heart that if this is what God wanted me to do with my life, then it would work out somehow. I let go of things so much that I felt as if I didn't even care if it worked out or not. Later that evening, as I was sitting in my kitchen talking to my Husband, my phone dinged. It was my Aunt texting me to see if I wanted my Cousin Kevin's old rocking chair to give to my Daughter, which I thought was so sweet of her to offer us, because her son Kevin had passed away some years before at the age of 27 in a drunk driving motorcycle accident. Honored to accept it, I suggested we meet up tomorrow morning over coffee so that I could grab it from her. She agreed to meet.

The next morning we met at a café, ordered coffee, found a table. and sat down for a chat. Right away I noticed that my Aunt was wearing a shirt with a compass on it, and compass earrings. My first thought was to tell her about the Mindful Heart Project, but I didn't. Just last night I had turned it completely over to God and I wasn't trying to find the money anymore. We talked about family, and life, and what we've been up to, and careers. This lead me to make conversation about how I really wanted to find a way to help people for a living and the next words out of her mouth made me want to fall out of my chair. She said to me, "YOU SHOULD WRITE A BOOK." I sat there in total disbelief, unable to say anything for a moment thinking about how I should respond. I decided that this was too much of a sign for me not to say anything any longer. I told her about the book writing program, the Mindful Heart Project, and the compass logo. She was shocked by all of the coincidences and synchronicities. I told her about the cost of the program, but still didn't ask for the money. I was done asking people for the money, and honestly I didn't want to make my Aunt feel awkward for having to say no to me. I switched the conversation back to something else and we finished our coffees.

When our cups were empty, she said that she'd meet me next to my car with the rocking chair. I pardoned myself to use the restroom saying that I'd be right out when I was done. As I walked toward my car, my Aunt was walking toward me and said "What if I ask your Uncle if he'd be willing to let you borrow the money to write this book? I really feel like this is your calling in life. The coffee company I wasn't so sure about, but I feel this is what you are meant to do." I could not believe what I was hearing. There standing in front of me was my Aunt offering me the $14,000 I needed to bring my book, and my coaching practice; the Mindful Heart Project to life... and I didn't even ask for the money.

The next day I hopped on the final interview call for the program, was accepted, and given an offer to join. Because of my Aunt, and God, I was able to enroll in the program, write this book, and offer you the option to keep working with me directly to dive even deeper into evolving and growing your soul through the Mindful Heart Project.

The lesson in all of this is that there is an incredible amount of power and opportunity that comes when you turn your life completely over to God, because once you do, that is when God is able to do his best work for you without any resistance from you. When we resist God, it's similar to a toddler having a temper tantrum thinking that they know best. Trusting God 110% is not a weakness, it's a strength, and once you begin to do it, your life will get easier and incredible things will happen for you too. Trust me on this one.

ACKNOWLEDGEMENTS

It took a team of people to help me write this book, all of whom I want to acknowledge and thank for their special contribution.

First I'd like to thank my Mother for encouraging me throughout my life to reach for my dreams no matter how crazy or far-fetched they may have sounded. Thank you for watching Lenora each week so that I could give this book the attention it needed and deserved. It's because of you that I was able to write it, and it will help so many people. There's absolutely no way that I could have done do this without you. I love you.

Aunty Sharon and Uncle Gilly. Thank you for believing in my gift of healing and for knowing that my calling in life is to help people grow and evolve. I wouldn't have been able to write this book without your support and for that I am eternally grateful. Aunty Sharon, you are my Angel, and I know that your soul and my soul planned this long before we were born because the signs were everywhere. I love you both very much.

Phil. Thank you for your support whenever and however you could give it. You are a good man, a great Father, and a wonderful Husband. I love you.

Tara. You're a beautiful soul and I want to thank you for opening up your world and heart to me. You've been through so much and in being vulnerable and brave enough to share everything with me, you've educated and inspired me in ways you'll never realize. It makes my heart happy to know that your world is looking up and that you're managing your recovery like a boss each and every day. I love you.

Holli Lamb-Melville. Thank you for watching Lenora while I worked on this book. It takes a village and you are a great friend for helping me to make it happen. I love you.

Dr. Angela Lauria. You've worked so hard to create a business that is giving natural born healers everywhere a way to amplify their voice in order to help others. Your process helped me to pull out of my heart, and my head, all of the things I've been wanting to say for so long. For that I thank you and have so much love for you.

To God, Jesus, my Angels, and Spirit Guides. I know you've been there the whole time helping everything to align ever so perfectly. Thank you for the signs, synchronicities, and messages. I hope you are proud of the work I've done in the name of spreading God's unconditional love and light out into the world. I love you all.

ABOUT THE AUTHOR

Nicole Molloy is an Author, Spiritual Wellness Mentor, and Coach. She helps addicts in recovery to create a life they love by transforming their life through spirituality and mindful thinking techniques in order to overcome the deeply rooted, highly destructive patterns of self-sabotage.

Since she was a young child, Nicole has possessed a psychic level intuitive gift known as "Claircognizance" or "clear knowing." This gift has allowed her to receive and understand a complex collection of insights from her Guides and Angels about how and why people sabotage their happiness, success, and relationships with others-- and how to fix it.

This continuous communication has turned the last 30 plus years of her life into a study of the human condition; observing the world from outside of herself, from an objective perspective. Inspired by these interactions, Nicole has been a philosopher of spirituality and psychology for most of her life.

There was a time when Nicole kept this powerful collection of insights quietly to herself, until one day, God made it understood that it was time to share her knowledge with the people of the world who are feeling lost or stuck in their lives, and want to make a change.

She accepted the challenge, and in doing so, made a complete career switch from marketing to life coaching. A move which she hopes will inspire people to be brave in their mission to stay true to themselves.

Along with a Master of Science in Marketing, Nicole possesses a Master Practitioner Certificate in Neuro-Linguistic Programming (NLP), Cognitive Behavioral Therapy (CBT), and Life Coaching.

She lives in Massachusetts with her husband Phil, daughter Lenora, son AJ, and Bulldog, Otis.

THANK YOU

Thank you to everyone who believed in themselves enough to read this book. You are beautiful souls who have very valuable lessons to learn in this lifetime, and very important roles to play in the lives of others.

To show my gratitude to you I want to give you a free getting started guide that I've created titled "The Five Things You Need To Do To Prepare For A Spiritual Journey." Simply go to this link https://www.nicolemolloy. com/fivethings/ enter your email and I'll send a copy of it to your inbox.

Made in the USA
Monee, IL
19 December 2019